SENSIBLE SMALL BUSINESS ADVERTISING

SENSIBLE
SMALL BUSINESS
ADVERTISING

Successfully Building Your Business
with Effective Advertising

JACK STEPHENS

iUniverse LLC
Bloomington

SENSIBLE SMALL BUSINESS ADVERTISING
SUCCESSFULLY BUILDING YOUR BUSINESS WITH EFFECTIVE ADVERTISING

iUniverse books may be ordered through booksellers or by contacting:

iUniverse
1663 Liberty Drive
Bloomington, IN 47403
www.iuniverse.com
1-800-Authors (1-800-288-4677)

Because of the dynamic nature of the Internet, any web addresses or links contained in this book may have changed since publication and may no longer be valid. The views expressed in this work are solely those of the author and do not necessarily reflect the views of the publisher, and the publisher hereby disclaims any responsibility for them.

Any people depicted in stock imagery provided by Thinkstock are models, and such images are being used for illustrative purposes only.

Certain stock imagery © Thinkstock.

ISBN: 978-1-4759-9499-5 (sc)
ISBN: 978-1-4759-9500-8 (hc)
ISBN: 978-1-4759-9501-5 (e)

Library of Congress Control Number: 2013910827

Printed in the United States of America.

iUniverse rev. date: 8/6/2013

CONTENTS

ARE YOU OUT OF YOUR MIND?

GETTING STARTED

This book is a much-needed tool for both small business owners and people who are considering starting their own business. In these times of economic difficulty, there are more and more people in that category, but I want you to think of this book as written with just *you*, personally, in mind.

John Wanamaker, a highly successful department store magnate of the mid-1800s, said, "Half the money I spend on advertising is wasted. The trouble is I don't know which half." These days there is no reason to have that same thing happen to you, yet here we are, a century and a half later, and I find businesses who needlessly struggle with that same dilemma.

I looked long and hard to find anything that even remotely approaches the subject matter and information I have compiled here for you, and I came up pretty empty. Although some of the concepts and principles I am sharing with you are found in bits and pieces on the Internet or scattered about in a variety of sources, there was no single resource where these ideas were available until now.

What you will find in these pages is unique in its emphasis and in its ability to provide you with essential direction to help you start or correct the course of your advertising campaign.

My approach is going to be very casual and a bit folksy at times, as if you and I are conversing on a one-to-one basis. No ivory towers or dry textbook reading allowed.

If you are already a business owner, I will probably step on your toes and maybe even make you angry. If so, I offer this advice: Get over it! Forget what you think you know. Try to remove your experiences, good and bad, from the primary place in your thinking about advertising. This will be tough. We human beings are wired to interpret the world through the lens of personal experience.

But our experiences are based on perceptions, and perceptions—no matter how strongly we are influenced by them—can be wrong. The problem is that we will hold on to them regardless of the truth because it is what we *want* to believe.

I did *not* say that I want you to ditch your experiences altogether. I merely want you to allow something else—a wider base of research, observation, and experience—to interpret *your* experiences, guide your thinking, and correct your perceptions.

The most difficult people I have ever had to deal with have been business owners with a know-it-all attitude. I remember a travel agent I stopped in to talk to. He had no use whatsoever for the particular product lines I was offering. Yet he had no idea what those product lines were. He had no interest in seeing what facts, figures, demonstrations, and customer testimonials I could have shared with him.

In his mind, there wasn't a soul out there who was benefiting from my company's products. I guess he figured that my company's longevity and success had occurred without our having created any business for anyone. As far as he was concerned, the only advertising product of my type that was effective was my competitors'.

Now, I had no problem with my competitors' products. If they weren't making a profit for their clients as well, they wouldn't exist. But I knew that my company offered better products at a better price. It was easier for my advertisers to get a good return on their investment with my product lines than with my competitors' higher-priced products.

My advice to the travel agent (had he cared to listen) would have been to set a reasonable budget for that type of advertising and split it between both companies. I'll share more on this concept later.

Back to my discussion with the agent. His perception was skewed by his own opinion based on very little experience and no hard facts. I always keep my cool in situations like that, but inwardly I was thinking, *You dolt! Your mind is so made up, you don't want to be bothered with the facts.* Never mind that I had hundreds of satisfied clients who were getting lower-cost leads every day through my company. Never mind that I had plenty of those customers who had vouched for the great results we had produced for them. Never mind that we had a great tracking program that offered an accurate system to verify every lead we generated.

There are times when I wish I could just say, "You know, you're right. Our advertisers don't get any business from us. They just continue, year after year, to buy useless, ineffective advertising from us because they like us so much. And they do it without receiving any benefit whatsoever from us."

Sarcastic? You betcha. And you can also bet that if you communicate that travel agent's attitude to me, I'm thinking the same thing about you and wishing I could say the same thing to you. Problem is, the only safe place to say that kind of thing is somewhere like here, in the pages of this book.

Every single word I am writing is meant to *help you succeed,* so just take my occasionally abrasive approach as tough love and keep a sense of humor about it. Or pass this book on to someone else who *will* follow my advice. In fact, give it to one of your competitors. *Someone* might as well benefit from it.

If you are a first-timer at starting a business, my first words of advice to you are to be teachable. I realize that there is an inherent feistiness in most entrepreneurs. That's great. You will need some gumption if you are going to tough it out during the early days, weeks, months—even years—of your business start-up.

But in the throes of the struggle to get going, don't allow yourself, whether due to fear or to arrogance, to reject guidance that may help you. Just as I said to the veteran business owners, put your preconceived notions, your opinions and perceptions, aside long enough to be instructed by someone who has been on the other side of the desk from where you are sitting. Gain insight and input from someone who has been in the advertising business for well over a decade and who is willing to give you an insider's counsel.

I don't know everything, but I do know *some* things. And they are things that need to be said and listened to by the business community. I have no ax to grind, no product to sell, no reason to steer you anywhere but down a reasonable path to success. So as I said, be teachable.

JUST WHO DO I THINK I AM?

Let me tell you why you should listen to me. Consider this: Suppose you have been in business for thirty-five years. That's thirty-five years of experience and experimentation regarding advertising. That's great. You've seen a lot of advertising variations come and go. You may have added and subtracted many types of advertising over those years, and that experience is very valuable, coming, as it does, from the school of hard knocks.

I started in this industry in 1999. Prior to that, I served in a position that gave me access to many small businesses and government officials. Since then, I have served the advertising needs of well over 1,500 businesses. Conservatively speaking, then, I have accumulated experience in helping a wide variety of businesses with different degrees of fiscal health, from brand new start-ups to large, well-established companies.

So let's see … your experience with one company over thirty-five years versus my experience over thirteen years helping more than 1,500 businesses. Who do you suppose has more overall experience? I'm not discrediting whatever knowledge you may have, but maybe I know a thing or two that will help you.

So whether you are just starting out or you are already in business and trying to make sense of advertising, I am hoping to share with you my expertise in the field to help you get started in advertising and to develop and grow your business successfully.

I am proud to say that I have helped many small businesses begin and/or flourish by providing them with effective advertising programs. I have counseled, developed ad campaigns, helped design logos and slogans, and advised on ad content and placement and on media choices.

In the process, I have gained the confidence and friendship of the clients I have served, whether they are sole proprietors or major corporations. They know that everything I have done for them is geared toward helping them succeed.

I'M ON YOUR TEAM

Years ago, when I was just getting started in my field, Russ Thomas, my very wise manager, gave me some of the best advice I have ever received. I was at a point where I had become concerned about whether I would be making enough at my job. He showed me that I was focusing on myself and my own needs. He knew that if I did that, I would end up selling only what would profit me the most, and at some point, I would be discouraged and probably defeated. End of career.

So he gave me this advice: "Jack, if you will just take care of your customers, they will take care of you." And from that day forward, that has been my philosophy. It sounds so simple, but it is tried and true. Unfortunately not everyone in the fields of advertising and marketing actually follow that principle. I know that if I concentrate on doing what is best for my customers, if I take care of my clients' needs, my needs will be taken care of in the process. Everybody wins.

My hope is that this tool will help you succeed. My purpose is to give you a missing and badly needed tool in the area of advertising and to do it solely with your benefit in mind.

Every small business owner I have encountered over the years has been unique. There are business owners who are a pleasure to deal with, and there are some who are mean as snakes. Some are proud and arrogant. Some are meek but serious go-getters. Some are complete neophytes regarding starting or running a business. Some are old hands who have perhaps started and run various businesses over the years. Yet they almost all share one thing in common.

Most know nothing about advertising, some know a little, a few know a lot, and way too many *think* they know everything. That last group is the hardest to deal with. I hope that isn't you. Actually, it probably isn't you, because if you think you already know everything about advertising, you won't be reading this.

I believe that I have seen an underlying characteristic in many of these fine people, whether it appears as arrogance or as caution. And that characteristic is fear. Fear of failure. A hesitance to commit to ideas or recommendations regarding advertising. If this fits your situation, please allow me the opportunity in these pages to give you the guidance to help you develop an effective advertising program. Stay focused and stay positive. So let's proceed.

DO YOU FEEL THE NEED? THE NEED TO SUCCEED?

New businesses spring up every day. Some will make it; some won't. Which group do you want to be in? If you don't plan and you don't make yourself aware of some of the pitfalls, you'll fall flat on your face. Maybe sooner, maybe later, but you will.

The following reasons for business failure are to be found on many Internet sites. I had intended to address each of these in some detail, but since others have already done so, I recommend that you take note of the reasons and research them further on your own so you and I can stay focused on the importance of advertising. I am including them here to make sure you address them. Advertising will make no sense if you allow fatal flaws in other areas of your business. As you set off on this grand adventure, avoid these mistakes:

1. No Business Plan. Whether you are already in business or not, I recommend that you take the time right now to *stop reading and spend time developing your business plan before you do anything else.* There are many sources to help you. Do a search online or check with your local small business development office or chamber of commerce. Consult SCORE (www.score.org) for tons of free counseling on anything with which you need help, including developing a business plan.

2. Starting a Business Only to Make Money. Making money should not be your only motivation. An additional good reason for starting a business is to provide a better product or service than is already out there. The drive to *do it better* propels the successful businessperson. Without some kind of mission, you'll be prone to flounder when the going gets tough.

3. Starting without Sufficient "Shoestrings." You are only asking for trouble by not knowing how much money your business will require, not only for start-up costs but also for the costs of staying in business. Planning for it and having your seed money in hand is essential.

4. Lack of Management Skills. This includes lack of relevant business and management expertise in areas such as financing, purchasing, selling, production, and hiring and managing employees.

5. Poor Location. If you are going to have a storefront or shop, in most cases you will need to pay for the privilege of a prime location. If the location has drawbacks, what will you do to overcome them?

6. Overexpansion. Growing too rapidly may lead to the inability to produce goods or services quickly enough to meet demand and/ or the inability to provide adequate customer service.

7. No Website. This is the twenty-first century, people. Every business should have a professional-looking, well-designed, and search-engine-optimized (SEO) website that enables users to easily find out about the business and avail themselves of the products and services. In fact, in the majority of cases, most businesses will center all their advertising on driving traffic to their website. I'll have more on this in a later section.

8. Ignorance of Your Competition. If you don't know who your competitors are, how long they have been around, what they do, how they do it, where they are, and even what their future plans are, how are you going to differentiate yourself from them? Your competition probably knows about you and is going to make sure they keep the upper hand.

9. Ineffective or Inadequate Marketing and Advertising. Learn how to advertise and promote your business in a cost-effective manner. The main purpose of this guide is to help you with this area of your business. So get ready. We are closing in on this area very quickly.

PRIMED FOR SUCCESS

Steve Blank, a professor at Stanford University, said that about 90 percent of start-ups die because they can't find their market.[1] So listen to what customers are saying, understand their needs, and find the way to explain exactly how you can meet those needs. Then *communicate that answer through your advertising program.*

Having read this far, are you ready to go on or are you beginning to reconsider the idea of starting or continuing your own business? Not everyone is cut out for running a business. Everyone who *wants* to have a business should not necessarily *have* a business. Some of those who have a business now are trying to run it by the seat of their pants without any clear idea of how it should be done. And quite often those people are too bone-headed to listen to advice or to seek help. Sad but true. Above all else, remember: *please be teachable.*

It has been my observation over the years that about 90 percent of the business owners I have dealt with have been *people in business*, but only about 10 percent of them have been *businesspeople*. There is a world of difference between the two. I hope you are in the latter group. So let's dive into the real reason why you picked up

---

1   http://www.p2w2.com/blog/index.php/top-5-reasons-why-small-businesses-fail/.

this book and begin looking at what you need to know to succeed in business through effective advertising.

Before we get into the nuts and bolts of the subject, let me ask you: Do you realize just how important your business is to our nation's economy?

SMALL BUSINESS: AMERICA'S TRUE DRIVING FORCE

According to the US Department of State's website, http://www.state.gov/, small businesses, defined as those with fewer than five hundred employees, account for more than half of the country's private-sector employment. Now that is impressive. That may be surprising to you if you hadn't considered it before. Don't you tend to think of the big guys, the GMs, the AT&Ts, the stock market giants, as the only real influences on the economy? Well, they aren't. You are.

In fact, Dr. Chad Moutray, chief economist for the Office of Advocacy, agrees that small businesses are job creators.[2] The US Office of Advocacy provided data and research showing that small businesses represent 99.7 percent of all firms. They create more than half of the private nonfarm gross domestic product, and they create *60 to 80 percent* of the net new jobs.[3] Small businesses account for *52 percent* of all US workers, according to the US Small Business Administration.[4] And according to the Federal Reserve

---

2   http://www.hudsonreporter.com/view/full_story/20898323/article-Kicking-off-the-holidays-Bayonne-joins-American-Express-in-Small-Business-Saturday-.

3   http://www.sba.gov/sites/default/files/sbfaq.pdf.

4   http://economics.about.com/od/smallbigbusiness/a/us_business.htm.

Board's National Survey of Small Business Finances (1995), small businesses were home-based *53 percent* of the time.[5]

HISTORY OF SUCCESS

Although many people believe that 80 percent of all small businesses fail within five years, statistics from the US Census Bureau reveal a different story. The Census Bureau reports that 76 percent of all small businesses operating in 1992 were still in business in 1996 and only 17 percent of all small business closings in 1997 were due to bankruptcies or other failures. Any other business closings were due to the business being sold or incorporated or the owner retired.[6]

Statistics from the Small Business Administration (SBA) show that "two-thirds of new employer establishments survive at lease two years, and 44 percent survive at least four years."[7] The belief that 50 percent of businesses fail in the first year is false. Brian Head, an economist with the SBA Office of Advocacy, noted that "as a general rule of thumb, new employer businesses have a 50/50 chance of surviving for five years or more."[8]

Do you want your business to be one of the survivors? Keep reading to discover the missing elements in your business's success and longevity.

---

5   http://www.tabsusa.com/Technology/Small-Businesses-Can-Achieve-More-Now-41.html.

6   http://www.videogameg.com/Smallbusiness.html.

7   http://www.networksolutions.com/smallbusiness/wp-content/files/sbfaq.pdf.

8   http://voices.yahoo.com/why-so-many-businesses-fail-part-2-11959093.html.

ADVERTISING 101

In preparation for starting a business, a mechanic learns how to repair cars. A doctor spends a lot of time and money getting an education and serving time as an intern. An attorney likewise has to invest in education, pass the bar exam, etc. Whether you are a roofer, plumber, retail store owner, or whatever else, from architect to zookeeper, somehow you learned how to do what you do.

Someone taught you how to effectively perform your service or produce your product. Someone probably even coached you on how to run the business, market your business, keep the books, take inventory, comply with regulations, hire employees, provide benefits, etc.

Whether this is your first venture into running your own business or you have been at it for years, you more than likely share one problem in common with almost every other business.

EXPAND YOUR EDUCATION

In spite of all the education, experience, training, apprenticeships, and seminars in which you have been involved to prepare you to succeed in business, there is one area that no one seems to prepare you for, and that missing element—that crucial part of enabling your success—is *learning how to advertise.*

No one sits you down and explains how to advertise, what forms of advertising are available, which ones will work best for you, what to expect from various forms of advertising, how to develop a successful advertising program, how to keep your advertising program working as effectively as possible, how to gauge the success of your advertising program, how to tweak the program as you go, etc.

Instead, you are at the mercy of every ad salesperson who comes through the door or who calls you on the phone. You will be prone to make your decision to either listen to them or to blow them off based only on whether or not you like them or how busy you are at the time or what kind of day you are having, or some other subjective "reason."

Now listen to this. This is very important. I know you won't want to hear this, but it is true. Refusing to take the time to hear what advertising salespeople have to offer is a big mistake. I know it takes time from your day. I know some of them grate on your nerves. I know you have heard from somebody that the ad product the salesperson wants to talk to you about "doesn't work."

I also know that *you* might not be Mr. or Ms. Congeniality yourself. Having been in this field for quite some time, I can tell you that it isn't easy being an advertising salesperson. Ad salespeople take a lot of abuse and usually have to do it with a smile. The more professional the salesperson, the less you'll notice just how ticked off he or she gets when you treat them rudely.

If you refuse to take the time to learn what is available to reach potential customers, you do so at your own peril. And in my judgment, that makes you—shall we say—not very bright.

I am being charitable here. If you really can't take the time to listen, you had better hire someone (like me) who can, and then give them the authority to act on your behalf to sort through all the offers and build an advertising program for you.

I have dealt with businesspeople who seemed to believe that they knew more about advertising than I did. They may have cut me off before I could get into my presentation. They may have bad-mouthed my product. They may have even attempted to insult my intelligence.

There are reasons why I could endure such treatment. I knew that sometimes the businessperson was just ignorant about advertising. They were actually afraid—afraid of making a costly mistake or of appearing weak. They didn't want to get talked into something that wasn't going to help them. They may have thought that acting tough was part of the game to get a better deal. Or they may have tried the same type of ad program before and didn't get the results they thought they should. Regardless of the "reason," somehow they felt as if that gave them the right to think they knew more than I, a specialist in the field, knew. If that is your attitude toward the advertising salesperson, it is little wonder that you end up treating them badly.

I remember dealing with the wife of a man who owned an auto repair business. She handled all the advertising for the business, which would have made sense if she did it because her husband didn't have the time to deal with the advertising part of the business.

But at one point I asked her if it would be possible to meet with both him and her so we could benefit from his input. She said, "Oh, no. You'll never get to meet with him. He hates salespeople." To which I replied, "You mean he hates salespeople other than *him*, because he happens to be a salesman too. He sells tires, tune-ups, and other repairs, and I sell advertising to *help* him sell those things."

In any case, any time I was ever treated badly by a businessperson, I never came away thinking the businessperson was right or justified when I knew that I carried myself with integrity and professionalism. The situation just clarified for me what kind of person I was dealing with.

UNDERSTANDING YOUR AD SALESPERSON

Here is another subject you will probably never see anything written about anywhere else; that is, considering how you treat your advertising salesperson. Now, granted, there are salespeople out there who are not the best. This field is extremely difficult, and your hat should be off to those who are successful at it. I sometimes hear business owners say, "Yeah, I seem to have a different ad salesperson every year," as if that somehow reflects negatively on the advertising product or the advertising company. Actually it quite often has more to do with you, the businessperson, than you realize.

Advertising sales reps have a lot to deal with in their career. They are expected to be out there every day cold-calling, making presentations, learning more about their ever-expanding product line, researching the companies they are trying to help, meeting quotas for revenue retention, quotas for increase on existing sales, and quotas for new customers, dealing with customer-service issues, staying current with changes in their industry, and meeting goals for various types of advertising products.

The best of them are trying to match the needs of your business with the products they have to offer. The mediocre among them are at least trying to get you noticed to some degree.

But even in the worst of scenarios, those salespeople think that they are doing something to bring you more leads and more business. So why treat them as if they are looking for a hand-out or as if they are trying to steal your money?

They often are responsible for traveling thousands of miles a year to meet you and hundreds of others like you. You might be surprised to know how often ad salespeople travel to an appointment only to be stood up by the business owner who agreed to meet with them. They deal with no-show businesspeople who have no more respect or courtesy than to fail to keep their appointment without so much as a call in advance to tell them the meeting needed to be canceled or rescheduled—as if the salesperson's time, gas, and preparation were somehow worthless. You don't appreciate it when it happens to you, and neither do they. Senior sales reps know that it happens all the time and always will, but they still don't like it. They have learned to deal with it, and they are the ones who will survive. Others can't take it and leave to find some other career.

With the disrespect, poor treatment, broken appointments, constant travel, and challenges to justify the value of their product lines to you, is it any wonder that you may not get the same sales rep back the next year? Career longevity in this type of sales is difficult to achieve.

MAKE A FRIEND OF YOUR SALES REP

If you feel that you are dealing with a novice or someone who is not working for your best interests, or if you don't think you are getting the best product for your needs, consider asking the company for another rep. But as you are doing this, have some consideration for the difficult job the rep has, and remember that even the newest of them should be trying to help your business. There is never any justification in treating these salespeople badly.

In fact, you should greet them with open arms and be interested in seeing what the latest developments and product offerings are. Instead of putting off your meeting with them, make it an important priority. Deal with them sooner rather than later. Never break an appointment with them unless you have to, and never do it without giving them the courtesy of a call in advance to reschedule.

These people are here to *help you make money*. Why in the ever-lovin' world would you allow them to form a negative opinion of you? You should make best buddies of them. Without customers, your business is dead. When someone is trying to help you attract customers, that is a *good thing*. I always think of myself as a partner in my clients' businesses. When I drive down a street, I take pride in being able to point out the businesses I serve and say, "That one is mine. And that one. And that one …" because I know that, to some degree, I have a part in their success.

Every advertising product has its place and is effective in some way. It may not be a medium that you will use, but each product, if used correctly and with the right expectation, works for someone. If it didn't work at all for anyone, it wouldn't exist. Just as it is with your business, if no one uses your product or service, you'll cease to exist.

So when someone says they tried a certain type of advertising and it didn't work, I have a pretty good idea that they either had the wrong expectation about the kind of result they should have had or they didn't know how to use the medium most effectively.

Whatever the medium, ad salespeople are convinced of your need for their particular form of advertising. Their conviction may only be fueled by their need to meet a sales quota, or it may reflect a genuine concern to help you. Usually, your response will be one of the following.

NOT YOUR TYPE?

You may be so turned off by the demeanor or personality of the ad salesperson that you decide not to give them a hearing. The better course of action would be to call the company and request another sales rep.

Remember that you and the advertising sales rep are supposed to be on the same team. You both want your business to succeed. If you don't get this vibe from your rep, get another one. But don't rob yourself of knowledge and tools just because you don't like someone.

THE REMEDY FOR FEAR

You may decide whether to participate in some form of advertising or not on the basis of your own, or someone else's, previous experience. You may think that whatever the advertising product is, you don't need it, or it won't work for you. One way or another, your decision-making process may be influenced by fear: fear of failure.

Was your decision a sound one? What if your preconceived notion about the effectiveness of the medium is wrong? A person's bias wields a very strong power over what they think is true, whether it is or not. But what if there really isn't anything "wrong" with the type of advertising? What if the problem is that you (or whoever it was that coached you in your opinion) either didn't use the ad product in the right way or had the wrong idea of what to expect from the product? Are you afraid of losing money instead of making money in the process?

If you don't see the results you expected from your advertising, you'll be prone to just write the medium off and declare that it just "didn't work" for you. You'll figure that somehow your business is "different" from all other businesses and therefore the more conventional ways of advertising just don't work for you. Sometimes there may be some truth to this, but not nearly as often or as much as you may think. Quite often the problem is that you had the wrong expectation for the medium you used.

On the other hand, you may decide that what the salesperson shows you makes total sense and you may invest in that product. Even in this case, you'll be cautious in evaluating the results. There's no doubt that, as with any investment, it will involve some level of risk.

MIND-ALTERING CONCEPTS

Sometimes we have to change our way of thinking to correct problems. I truly hope I can get you to change your way of thinking in order to remedy the frustrations you may have had in your attempts to advertise.

One of the main changes you have to make is this: *stop thinking like a business owner and start thinking like a potential customer.* Too many business owners base their choices of advertising media on price alone. "What is cheapest? What is the *absolute least amount* I can pay for advertising?"

And yet, you are the same people who will steer your customer away from a lower-cost item toward a higher-priced one. Why? I hope it isn't just because it will bring you a higher profit. I hope it is because you know that, penny for penny, the higher-priced item excels in performance, durability, ease of use, etc. The higher-priced item is a better value for your customer and is, therefore, worth the difference in price.

One of my advertising clients, a law firm, had a yellow-page phone-book ad campaign consisting of a small, one-inch in-column ad under the main heading of "Attorneys." One of the lawyers who was influential in deciding their ad campaign declared that the office hadn't received "any calls" from their ad.

Well, duh! Look in any phone book and you'll see exactly why the ad didn't accomplish much. Their ad was far too miniscule to have any major impact compared to page after page of full-page ads run by other attorneys. Does it take big bucks to advertise that way? You bet it does!

Look at all the other firms who do it year in and year out. Why? Because they know that the investment brings them exposure and business. Do you suppose lawyers just love throwing their advertising money around regardless of whether they get a return on their investment? Not the lawyers I know.

This is where your skull may tend to get a little thick. Somehow you don't see how that principle applies to *your* advertising. So you underinvest in advertising and then complain because your advertising "didn't work." More important than price is the quality and the return on investment that the advertising will bring you.

Stay with me and be patient. I do have your best interests at heart. If you haven't thrown this book across the room yet, keep reading.

ADVERTISING: THE MISSING LINK

The most fundamental reason for business failure is lack of sales, which is caused by—are you ready for this? This is really earthshaking—*lack of customers.* So let's talk about how to generate customers.

I've seen many businesses struggling to make a profit without advertising or without having a clear plan for their advertising. They are usually the first ones to complain that advertising "doesn't work."

I have run across business owners who have told me that they never advertise and, in spite of that, they are always busier than they want to be. As an advertising salesperson, when I hear that statement it tells me two things about those businesspeople.

It tells me, in most cases, that they are ignorant and/or arrogant. They are ignorant because they don't realize that there has never been any business anywhere that hasn't advertised in some way. If they have a sign on their shop or on their property, if they have word-of-mouth referrals, if they have lettering or a magnetic sign on their vehicle, if they place their business cards around town, they are advertising. In fact, there is no way on earth that a business can survive if that company doesn't advertise.

What they usually mean is that they just don't want to consider what the advertising salesperson has to say. They assume that they don't need whatever service or product is being offered. They mean that they don't want to spend (i.e., invest) money on advertising.

The arrogance comes in when they give me that haughty know-it-all look that tells me that they just don't want to consider doing anything differently than they already do. They feel that they are successful enough with the status quo or they believe they know all there is to know about advertising. I've even encountered the occasional businessperson who will point out how they have more business without advertising than some other businesses who *do* advertise. Again, ignorance and arrogance.

They seem to be of the opinion that *paid* advertising doesn't work. They don't want to spend (invest) any money to advertise because they don't think it is necessary. Or they might mean that they tried some form of advertising and it didn't do what they thought it should have; therefore, they conclude that it didn't work. They seem totally oblivious to the fact that they could have been farther along in their business success if they had invested in a program of well-planned advertising.

If the business owner has been in business for a while, they actually get peacock-proud of how they succeeded without all that "stuff." Never mind that some of their competitors may have survived, gone farther, grown larger, sold more, and had an easier time of it by advertising.

Businesses fail with and without advertising, but the survival rate is dramatically higher for a business that knows how to *effectively* advertise. Look at the history of businesses during the Great Depression. According to the OSM Blog (Open Sky Media, January 28, 2009) in an article titled "Companies That Survived the Great Depression,"

> Those companies who not only survived but did well and grew during the Great Depression are those who continued to act as though there were nothing wrong and that the public had money to spend. In other words, they advertised … [A]dvertising was the main factor in the growth or downfall of companies during those years.

The same goes for times of economic recession. As has often been said, "When times are good you *need* to advertise; when times are tough you *have* to advertise!"

Unfortunately, the opposite is what too many businesses do. I have heard business owners say, "When I make more money, then I'll advertise." Others have said, "I have to cut costs, so I am cutting back on my advertising." Still others have said, "I make enough money now. I don't need to advertise." Every one of those statements is foolhardy. As B. J. Palmer, one of the founders of the Palmer School of Chiropractic, said, "Early to bed, early to rise, work like h___, and advertise!" If you have to cut costs, cut costs; but don't cut investments. To cut your advertising is to cut off the lifeblood of your business. It is your direct artery to customers.

COUNTING THE COST

There are few resources that give the benefits and drawbacks for advertising media. Most resources address the advantages of each medium, but when it comes to the negatives or limitations of each, I have seen some of them conclude that every form of advertising is "too expensive."

Excuse me? Too expensive? What do you mean by *expensive*? If you mean that it is unnecessary or optional because it costs too much, you are wrong. If I want to start a parcel delivery business and need to choose a vehicle for my deliveries, a brand-new van may be too expensive for me, but if I don't plan to purchase some sort of vehicle, I'm out of business before I ever get started. Such a purchase is a necessary part of my business plan.

In the same way, advertising should be seen as a necessity—not as an unnecessary option—to doing business. You must have a vehicle to deliver the message of your business. You may not be able to start out with the most high-powered vehicle, but you do need something to convey your message.

If by expensive you mean the return on investment isn't what you expected, are you sure you had the proper expectation? The truth is that any advertising you choose will have some degree of success, whether you see it directly in sales or not.

If you buy business cards and give them out freely, placing them on countertops and tacking them to bulletin boards, you shouldn't expect a flurry of activity from them, but if you get one sale occasionally, you may find the return on the investment to be sufficient.

If you purchase advertising on your local television or radio station and you don't receive a large number of calls, was it worth it? Your investment was far greater than business cards on countertops, and you may not have "seen" anything happening from it. Was it a waste? If you thought it was, you had the wrong expectation. Did you have a call to action in the commercial? Did you provide location and contact information?

Your broadcast media commercial reached a far larger audience with a far more detailed message than your little pile of business cards could ever reach. You built an awareness of your business in the minds of an entire community. And you reached a wide range of potential customers, some of whom may turn into future customers. But you have to run your commercial for a long period of time to get the *top-of-mind awareness* you want. Repetition is one of the keys to success with the forms of advertising known as *creative advertising*. I'll have more on this later.

So which is better, the business card approach or the broadcast media approach? Actually, both are effective in their own ways. Know what to realistically expect from each one, and know how to estimate the return on your investment for the advertising you use.

DETERMINING YOUR RETURN ON INVESTMENT

Your advertising program should include many different forms of advertising, because you will find that the business cards and the broadcast media and your yellow-page ads or billboards or whatever else you decide to use all work together to bring the customer to the point of sale.

When evaluating each of the media in your advertising, one important consideration should be your *return on investment (ROI):*

- How much did you have to spend to get that lead?
- How many leads do you convert into customers? (And are you doing your best to convert those leads?)
- How much is a customer worth to you (based on your average profit per customer)?
- Was the cost of the lead less than the profit you made from the lead?
- Is your return on investment adequate to justify using the advertising medium?
- Is the return measurable? If it isn't, are you sure you want to invest in that particular form of advertising?

DO THE MATH

A simple formula for determining *return on investment* is this:

1. How many leads (phone calls, e-mail inquiries, in-store visits) from the advertising medium you are measuring does it take to sell one customer? Does it take three leads to convert one of those leads into a customer? Then put down "3" as your answer here.

2. What is your annual average profit per customer, including repeat business? This is what the average customer is worth to you. Jot down that figure. Let's say the average annual profit you receive from a typical customer, including repeat business during that year, is $1,200. (That's $100 per month, or $25 per week. For our formula, let's stick with the annual figure for all computations.)

3. What is the annual cost of the particular advertising medium you are measuring?

4. Since you want your advertising to do more than just pay for itself, what percent beyond this annual ad cost do you need to receive for your advertising expenditure to be worthwhile? Is it 10 percent? 25 percent? 50 percent? Be realistic and fair. A bank might give you 3 or 4 percent on money you invest there.

For example, if your annual ad cost is $3,600 and if you need to get an additional 25 percent for your ad program to give you a proper return, then multiply the annual ad cost by 125 percent. The result would be $4,500. (Your annual profit on the advertising will be $900.)

5. Divide the calculated amount in step 3 (ad cost plus ad profit) by the average customer profit figure you wrote down in step 2. In

this case we are dividing $4,500 by $1,200. The result is 3.75 leads converted to customers per year. Let's round that to 4.

6. Now multiply the number of leads (calls, e-mails, etc.) you need to acquire as a customer (from step 1) by the number of sales you need per year and you'll be able to determine how feasible it is to expect a certain return on the investment of your advertising dollars. In this case, it takes three leads to generate one sale, times four sales from the ad, so the annual number of leads the ad needs to produce is twelve. That's one customer lead a month.

Here is a simple worksheet for these calculations:

RETURN ON INVESTMENT (ROI) FORMULA

1. **How many leads do you need from your ad in order to generate one customer?**____

2. **What is your average annual profit per customer?** ____

3. **What is the annual cost for the ad?**____

4. **Take your ad cost from #3 and multiply by the percentage of additional profit you need to receive from the ad:** ____

5. **How many customers do you need to generate in order to receive the ROI you figured in #4? Divide line 4 by line 2:** _

6. **How many leads (calls, in-store visits, etc.) do you need to generate annually from the ad to realize your return on investment? Multiply line 5 by line 1:** ____

Now, is your advertising investment realistic? In many cases you may be surprised by how reasonable it is to invest in a particular ad program. If you are too "cheap" to invest in this way, you are only hurting yourself. And you'll probably struggle to survive.

By the way, if we are talking about converting leads into sales, remember that your advertising can only bring the inquiry or the lead to you. It is up to you and whoever answers the call or interacts with the potential lead to convert the contact into a customer.

So don't blame your advertising program if it brings you the contact, only to have you lose it because you lack the skills to convert the call into business or because you have an inept person dealing with the lead or because the calls all go to voice mail or because you allow the e-mail inquiry to go unanswered for too long. If you aren't good in this area, find someone who is to handle the leads for you.

SUMMING UP

So is the ad worth doing? Is a lead or two a month a reasonable expectation from the type of advertising you are doing? And just as importantly, are you accurately tracking the results to substantiate the expectation? No one can guarantee any particular results, but there should be a way to determine the likelihood of the results to be expected. Ask your ad rep for data to back up the effectiveness of the program you are being shown.

If you are going to follow my advice, pay close attention to the way you track the results. When I ask businesses to describe their means of tracking advertising results, most of them tell me that they ask everyone who calls, comes in, or contacts them by whatever means the question "Where did you hear about us?" For some forms of advertising this may suffice, but for phone calls in particular, you need to ask an additional question.

You will often find that more than one of your advertising media worked together to bring the lead to the point of contacting you, so if the contact came by way of a phone call, you will want to ask not just "Where did you hear about me?" (a sign, a word-of-mouth referral, etc.) but also "Where did you find my phone number?" If you use a form that asks "Where did you hear about me?" make the answer area open to multiple answers by using a "Check all that apply" approach.

There is no single magic bullet in advertising. If there were, everyone would be using that bullet and nothing else. You need a well-selected variety of weapons in your advertising arsenal.

If you are tempted to think that some form of advertising doesn't work, remember: if it wasn't working for anyone, that form of advertising wouldn't exist. No one would use it and it would go away.

Having the wrong expectation for a particular type of advertising may cause you to think it is not working. This is usually not true, but I'll have more on this in the chapters to come.

For now, just keep in mind that you shouldn't let your own personal opinion about the usage of any particular form of advertising be your gauge. Not everyone thinks or acts like you, and their buying habits don't necessarily mimic yours.

You aren't selling to yourself, so get out of the habit of using yourself as the measure of a medium's effectiveness. This is crucial.

You've heard of thinking outside of the box? Well, in this case *you are the box*. Get used to thinking outside of yourself and your buying habits. If you only target people who think and act like you do, you'll be limiting your potential customer base.

Start at whatever level of investment is workable for you, but don't make the mistake of considering advertising as an unnecessary expense. *Remember: advertising is the lifeblood of your business.*

TOO EXPENSIVE?

Going back to the misconception that advertising is too expensive, consider this: If your partners told you that they wanted to use some of your start-up money to buy a pretty picture to hang in the office and it would only cost $3,600, what would you say? "Are you crazy? We can't spend that kind of money on something like that!"

Why would you say that? Do you really want to hurt their feelings? Don't you appreciate fine art? After all, the picture is really beautiful. Rich colors, very artistic use of shading, interesting subject matter—a real eye-catcher! So what would be your objection? I hope you would tell your partners that it is unnecessary. It does nothing to add to your profit.

But what if that partner came to you and said that he or she had found an investment with the potential of giving you two or three dollars (or more) back for every dollar you put into it, and according to your partner's research, most successful businesses were investing in it and were seeing a very decent return on the investment.

In fact, while some businesses were getting a little less than two dollars, most were getting more, and some were getting far more. Would you consider investing some of your start-up money in that way? Two bucks back for every one you put in? How about if you could only get a buck and a half back for every one dollar you invested? Would you still think it was worth doing? Of course you would. You'd be nuts not to. That's what a properly built advertising program can do for your business.

INVESTMENT OR EXPENSE?

Advertising is not too expensive. In fact, advertising is not an expense at all. It is *not* one of your overhead costs. It is an investment—an investment in the success of your business. Some advertising will take more of an investment than others, and the return on your investment may vary from medium to medium, but the whole reason for each form of advertising is to *make you money!*

The truth is, you can't afford *not* to advertise. Remember that simple axiom if you are ever tempted to say that times are tough and you can't afford to advertise. The businesses who put the ax to their advertising when they are trying to trim back in order to survive are just making life harder in the process.

When times are stable, you need to advertise. When times are tough, you need to advertise even more. You have to compete harder for the fewer dollars that are out there.

A cartoon circulated around an advertising office a while back. The picture showed a king leaving his tent near the front lines of a battlefield. His knights and soldiers were hotly engaging the enemy, using swords and spears in the desperate struggle. The king was frowning and holding up a hand to fend off one of his advisors who was trying to direct his attention to a salesman standing outside the tent. The king angrily declared, "No, I can't be bothered to see any crazy salesman! We have a battle to fight!" If he had only turned and paid attention to the salesman, he would have seen that the salesman was trying to sell him—a machine gun!

Instead of seeing the salesman as an ally who wanted to aid him in his fight, the king thought of him as an unnecessary nuisance and a hindrance to his goal.

One of the frustrations I have had to face when selling advertising is the attitude of businesspeople who don't understand that advertising is not money *spent*. It is money *invested* to make them a profit.

SENSIBLE SMALL BUSINESS ADVERTISING 37

I have seen the attitude when I would walk into their place of business and observe their eyes glazing over and the smile on their face fading, or they hit me with "I'm not interested" before I had even shown them what I had to offer, or they act as if I am asking for a hand-out. I never mind a businessperson telling me no as long as they have given me the opportunity to show them what they are saying no to. At least I can then say that they had their chance and they threw it away, like the king in the cartoon.

So the next time you get a call from someone trying to sell you advertising, take advantage of the opportunity to see what they have to offer. Remember: educate yourself. There are choices you'll have to make. No one can do every form of advertising that comes along, but you owe it to yourself to see the salesperson as a *friend and potential partner* toward your success rather than someone who is just trying to part you from some of your hard-earned money. There are scams out there, and later I will address that subject, but don't reject the legitimate products with the scams. My momma would call that throwing out the baby with the bath water.

Of course the salesperson wants you to buy his or her product, and some may be more persuasive than others, but the ball is in your court. You determine which advertising you are going to buy. You may have to face some hardsell at times, but it is better to listen, evaluate, and make an informed decision than it is to wimp out and refuse to listen just because you don't have the guts to say no if you don't think the offered product is right for you.

Don't discard the product without first determining if it fits your need. The product is working for others. Why not consider that it might also work for you? Whether or not you utilize the advertising product or service is a choice you'll have to make, but it should be an informed choice, not a prejudgment, blind guess, or a final judgment on the effectiveness of the medium.

The money you budget for advertising is an investment—one of the most important parts of your business plan.

WILL IT WORK?

I have sometimes heard a businessperson say, "We tried [some form of advertising] and it didn't work." I am reminded of a joke about a man who walks into a hardware store and tells the salesman that he needs to cut down a large number of trees and needs a good tool to help him do it as efficiently as possible.

The salesman tells him that he has just the thing for him and directs him to a good, sturdy chainsaw. So the guy buys the chainsaw and walks out, happy as a lark.

The next day the man is back in the store, carrying the chainsaw, which is very badly beaten up. The blade is bent, the chain is hanging off, and the man is mad at the salesman for selling him that piece of junk. He says it took him even longer to cut down just one tree with the saw than it would have with his old ax.

So the salesman, puzzled about what had happened, takes the saw, straightens the blade, tightens the chain back up, and then proceeds to pull the starter cord. The saw tries to start with a "Brrbrrbrr," and the customer jumps back and says, "What was that?!" He obviously didn't know how to operate the saw. He was using it improperly and didn't get the result he thought he should.

When a businessperson tells me that he tried some advertising medium and it didn't work, that tells me that the businessperson didn't understand how to use the advertising medium or that he had the wrong expectation of what that medium was meant to do. He probably believed, as I have warned you against, that there is one magic advertising bullet, and boy, if he could just find it and use it—and it alone—well then, he would be assured of success. And he would live happily ever after. That attitude is exactly what it sounds like—a fairy tale. Wake up and get real.

BUILDING YOUR TEAM

AVOID THIS NEEDLESS CONFLICT

An unnecessary adversary to some forms of advertising may be your marketing director, a marketing seminar speaker, or whoever else you may be listening to for marketing advice. By "unnecessary" adversary I don't mean nonessential or unimportant. The services and expertise of a good marketing representative could certainly help you. The problem arises when the marketing consultant places themselves in an adversarial stance regarding the field of advertising.

There is no need for a conflict between what marketing consultants do for you and what your advertising program should be doing. Marketing will help you build your brand, find your target market, and package yourself to attract the right customers.

When it comes to marketing, your gurus may know their stuff, but if they downplay the necessity of sufficiently budgeting for advertising, beware. It might just be that they are trying to justify their own existence at the expense of your advertising investment.

Effective marketing will get you ready for presentation to the public. Advertising will bring the public to you. Each plays an important part in making your business successful.

You don't save money by hiring someone to come in and slash your advertising program to pay for their marketing services. You may have just robbed "Peter Ad Campaign" to pay "Paul Marketing Exec." In fact, I am often tempted to believe that if you laid all these self-proclaimed marketing specialists end-to-end it wouldn't be a bad idea. Again, I am not referring to every marketing consultant, but just be aware of the potential for this needless conflict.

A sensible marketing expert will understand the need for utilizing the right advertising mix to bring your marketing to the public effectively. Marketing and advertising should work together, not in opposition, to get the job done. And never, never, never allow anyone to rob you of your common sense about what works in the real world.

If you are doing the job right, your marketing and advertising will work together to build your success. But there are times when I have encountered a business owner who has listened to someone in the area of marketing who placed all the emphasis on financing a marketing plan to the virtual exclusion of an effective advertising program.

Marketing is essential to building your brand and clarifying your niche in the market. But without properly planning your advertising campaign to deliver that message and product, you are in for an unnecessarily tough time.

So the next time you or your partner go to some marketing seminar, beware the speaker who downplays the necessity of budgeting for specific advertising or who discourages a particular form of advertising that you and others have been using with good success. Build your program with equal attention to both marketing and advertising, and invest in both areas.

In the real world, you should get whatever help you can to work out a marketing plan. It is my opinion that, if you can only invest in one of these areas, do your marketing on your own and put your first investment into a good advertising program.

THE TWO ESSENTIAL TYPES
OF ADVERTISING

Let's start with some basics. First, there are two types of advertising: *directional* and *creative*. Get to know these terms and understand clearly the differences between them. Each of the two types has specific strengths and limitations, and you will need a balance of both types to be effective. If you grasp this fundamental idea, you'll be way ahead of your competitors. I believe that this one concept is so important to your advertising success that I would say that *if you don't follow anything else I am telling you in this book, follow this one principle and you will succeed.*

Small businesses on a shoestring budget will be able to get the right start and will be able to increase their businesses. Larger businesses with deeper (advertising budget) pockets will be able to make better use of, and get a better return on, their advertising investment. What follows is a simple, clear explanation of the two types. These are not either-or categories; rather, they are both-and. You'll need both types to minimize your cost and efforts and maximize your success.

DIRECTIONAL ADVERTISING: WHERE ARE *CUSTOMERS* LOOKING FOR YOU?

When you advertise in the places where consumers look when they are in need of a product or service, you are advertising in a *directional advertising* medium. Think about where you and others look when you need a product or service and you don't know with whom you will do business. Where do you look? Where do others look who don't think exactly the same way you do? If you need a plumber, or an electrician, or a daycare provider, or a new computer, where do you look to find the information you need to choose and contact a provider?

The most common answers are online (Google, Yahoo, local search engines) or in the yellow pages. These are the media in the category of *directional advertising*. These media are the foundation, the root system, of your business advertising plan. They have the *broadest base of potential customers* because *everyone has access* to these resources and the users of these media are *prequalified buyers*. They are looking in these media because they have the need or desire and they are *ready to buy*. Build a good foundation here and the rest of your advertising will be much more effective. I cannot stress this enough!

Next, reverse the question …

CREATIVE ADVERTISING: WHERE ARE YOU LOOKING FOR CUSTOMERS?

The other type of advertising you need is called *creative advertising*. It includes all the forms of advertising wherein you, the business owner, are looking for customers. You are trying to place yourself in front of enough people in as many places as you can, hoping to catch the attention of those who may need your services. You are also trying to build name recognition (branding) strong enough to catch those who don't need you right now but who may remember you when the need arises. In the advertising/marketing world this is known as creating TOMA (top-of-mind awareness).

Some forms of creative advertising may be broad, while others may provide the capability of being more targeted toward those consumers who are most likely to need you.

In your creative advertising, you might want to include a specific enticement to encourage a more rapid response, such as a limited-time offer, a grand-opening special, a buy-one-get-one coupon or some other offer. This is known as the *call to action*.

Some of the media you will use are television, radio, yard signs, word-of-mouth referrals, newspapers, magazines, billboards, flyers, business cards, direct mail, and many others.

In some cases, such as direct mail, you may be able to target certain demographics to tighten your focus on specific potential clientele. The most elusive variable in targeting is catching the target customer at the peak of their interest, at the specific time they are ready to buy. By also covering your directional advertising base, you will have taken care of this ready-to-buy market. This is one example of the complementary relationship between your directional and creative advertising.

MIXING IT UP

You need a proper mix of directional and creative advertising media for maximum effectiveness in getting the customers you need to start and maintain your business and to keep it healthy and growing. So let's look at some of the most popular forms of advertising and evaluate them so you can make an informed choice.

First, remember the difference between *directional* and *creative* advertising. To review:

Directional advertising deals with those media your customers/ clients/patients commonly use to search for products and services. Ask yourself, *Where do I look for things when I need to purchase something? Where do others who don't necessarily think like me look?* If you find the answer to those questions, you will know what the directional advertising media are: online search sources and the print yellow pages.

Strong advantages to these sources are that they are available to everyone in your area and you are dealing with prequalified buyers. The people looking in these places aren't just browsing aimlessly. They have a purpose. They are already interested. They are ready to buy. No one looks at directional advertising media unless they have a specific need, and when they have the need, they also have the directional media on hand.

So what you need to do is make sure you are found there with a *presence and message strong enough* to draw the customer's attention and interest. If your business is one where there is lots of competition, expect to pay more to make a bigger splash than the competition, to catch your customers' attention and to communicate a compelling reason to do business with you.

Creative advertising involves everything a business does to locate customers and draw attention to your business. It involves branding yourself and building top-of-mind awareness with your target market. You are fishing for customers. You may be reaching a very general audience or you may have targeted a specific demographic. In either case, some of your target audience may never need or use your service or product, some may need you at some point but not right now, and some are either interested now or could become interested with the right motivation.

Examples of creative advertising are television, radio, direct mail, billboards, yard signs, word of mouth, flyers in doors or on windshields, and signs on your car or truck. In each case, you are placing your name and contact information in places where you hope people with a need for your services will see them. This is a good thing. You have absolutely no chance of getting business from someone if they don't find out about you somehow.

Do not make the mistake of doing only creative advertising or directional advertising. You need a combination of media from both categories.

Let's look at what might happen if you don't balance directional and creative advertising. Let's say Jones Plumbing invests all his money in billboards. His billboard shows a picture of a leaky pipe and has his logo and phone number on it. Thousands of people see his billboard as they drive by, but most of these people don't need a plumber at that time.

However, one commuter driving by is reminded by the billboard that he has that pesky leak at home that his wife has been complaining about for days. He makes a mental note to call a plumber, maybe even Jones Plumbing, when he gets home.

By the time he gets home, he may or may not remember the plumber's name or his phone number, but he has been prompted by the billboard to look the plumber up. So he grabs his phone book, or he goes online, and lo and behold, Jones Plumbing doesn't show up.

But Smith's Plumbing has a prominent ad presence, with good information, including that he has twenty-four-hour service, services the customer's area, offers guaranteed work and reasonable rates, and even offers a discount the customer can use.

Will the potential customer continue searching for Jones, or will he call Smith instead? In many cases, Mr. Jones's creative advertising will drive business to Mr. Smith due to Mr. Smith's directional advertising, for which Mr. Smith should thank Mr. Jones. I have had businesses tell me they know this has happened for them.

USE BOTH HANDS!

You can swing a baseball bat with one hand, can't you? But if you want to get the best results, you use both hands, right? Likewise, for the best results, use both directional and creative advertising elements in your advertising plan.

Whatever mix of directional and creative advertising media you choose, you will find that they work together. It may be that a phone book or online ad was all it took to have a customer call you. But often, the customer contact will come as a result of exposure to more than one of your ads. The customer has seen your TV commercial a number of times, has heard your radio spot, and has received your direct-mail piece more than once.

So when the customer is finally ready for your services and he or she finds you due to your directional advertising, you will find that all these elements worked together to bring you business.

To do only one or the other of these two advertising types will result in overspending and in limiting your results.

What Does Your Business "Tree" Look Like?

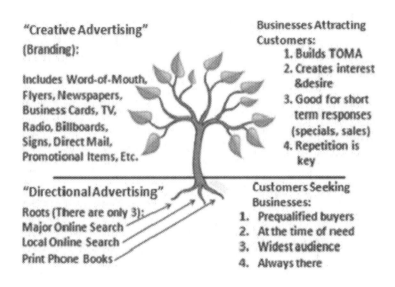

"Creative Advertising" (Branding):

Includes Word-of-Mouth, Flyers, Newspapers, Business Cards, TV, Radio, Billboards, Signs, Direct Mail, Promotional Items, Etc.

"Directional Advertising"

Roots (There are only 3):
Major Online Search
Local Online Search
Print Phone Books

Businesses Attracting Customers:
1. Builds TOMA
2. Creates interest &desire
3. Good for short term responses (specials, sales)
4. Repetition is key

Customers Seeking Businesses:
1. Prequalified buyers
2. At the time of need
3. Widest audience
4. Always there

Growing a Balanced Advertising Program

It might help to think of your business as a tree. Your business is the trunk of the tree, and the two types of advertising represent everything that supports and brings life to the trunk. The leaves on the tree represent all the creative advertising media, and the roots represent the directional advertising media.

To the right of the tree you will see a simple breakdown of some of the most common forms of advertising for each type. But remember that there are hundreds of creatives, just like there are hundreds of leaves on a tree. It would be hard to include them all on the graphic. The directionals are simpler in that there are only three categories to cover.

To the left of the tree are the main strengths of the two types. Note that even though both types exist to support and feed the tree, their strengths and results are not the same. They have different functions, just like a leaf doesn't do the same thing that a root does. Each has its own function. Both are necessary to the health and growth of the tree.

Your newspaper ad or flyer will never hit every possible consumer at the exact time of their need. Likewise, your phone book or Internet ad will not work well in building top-of-mind awareness (TOMA, #1 on the top left of the tree diagram) or in heralding a short-term sale. That would be like asking a root to carry on photosynthesis or a leaf to deliver fertilizer nutrients to the trunk. Just as you would not try to grow a tree with only leaves and no roots or vice versa, so you shouldn't try to grow your business without incorporating both types of advertising in your marketing program.

YOUR ROOTS: DIRECTIONAL ADVERTISING

YELLOW PAGES

Let's start with one of the oldest and most basic forms of directional advertising: the yellow pages.Yellow pages have less glamour and glitz than other forms of advertising, and there is a growing sense that the Internet will replace them altogether. But the reality is that the old standby of print yellow pages is far from dead and will probably never completely pass away. Yellow pages are the original search engine!

At a success seminar a few years ago (circa 2003), I remember hearing Paul Orfalea, the founder of Kinko's, asking the audience if they could name the most popular book in the world listing successful businesses. His answer was "the yellow pages." And even today, for most businesses, yellow-page advertising is still a foundational part of a well-rounded advertising campaign. With the shift to online sources, look for the rise of greater and greater bargains in print yellow-page advertising. If your business is solely online sales, this may not be the case.

Yellow pages require no electricity. They are printed on recycled paper, so they require less natural resources and less power to produce. They last longer and are more easily accessible than any other medium. In most cases, they are the fastest means of retrieving information. They are distributed over specific geographic areas to every business and home owner, regardless of how tech-savvy the recipient may or may not be. They blanket the area, and they are free to the consumer.

Granted, your ads will run into competition with every other business of your type that is also advertising, but if you aren't there, you've just relinquished the field to your competitors. And remember that the people looking you up are *prequalified buyers*. They wouldn't be looking under your headings if they weren't already interested in doing business. You just have to give them enough good reasons why they should choose to do business with you.

Since most standard yellow pages are printed once a year, you will need to make sure the ad information you place here is not time sensitive. This is obviously not the medium for announcing short-term sales or product offerings. When I build ads for restaurants, I recommend leaving prices out of yellow-page menu ads, or at least making sure there is a price-change disclaimer somewhere in the ad.

In temperate climates, a landscape contractor's work is fairly seasonal, with most of the jobs coming in the warmer months of the year. That is why many of them survive the slow winter months by offering snow-plowing service. Think in terms of the entire twelve months of the year when listing your business's services and products, and don't miss the opportunity to include those things you do throughout the year. If you are only thinking of the jobs you do when your ad sales rep is around, you may miss some strong buying information in your ads. You only have one go-around per year to get it right in the yellow pages, so make sure you do a thorough job.

Determine how many headings you belong under and place the most aggressive ads you can under every one of those headings. If that is beyond your means, take the list of related headings and prioritize them from the most relevant—the ones you absolutely *have* to be found under—to those with less importance. Then go down the list, covering as many as you can afford.

If you can't afford large display ads, buy the best you can afford. But buy *some* kind of ad space to tell your story. What you say will affect the response you get. A well-planned, smaller ad can have greater attracting power than a poorly planned, poorly worded larger ad. Later on I'll be sharing ad content guidelines.

If you have more than one yellow-page publisher in your area, talk to each one and use the better-priced offer from one as a bargaining chip to deal with the others. When the publisher has online products as well, expect to save on your program by purchasing a package deal containing both print and online elements at a savings.

Some phone-book publishers will be more willing than others to negotiate price. Ask about any incentive programs, introductory pricing, ad bundles, or other special offers that may be available to save you money.

Try to have some kind of ad presence in any phone books that cover areas where you want to do business. Don't fall for the song and dance given by some phone-book salespeople who declare that their book is the only one being used. It isn't true. All they are trying to do is bar you from spreading your budget out into a competitor's book. The other book wouldn't be there if no one used it. You will probably find that the competing book has much better rates than the one trying to pass itself off as the "only" book. So use the lower-cost program offered by one book to work a better deal with the other.

DIRECTIONAL ADVERTISING:
Where Customers Look for Businesses

ONLINE LOCAL SEARCH: INTERNET YELLOW PAGES

With the advent of online advertising, yellow-page publishers realized that they needed to find a way to represent their advertisers in this new medium. To do this they reproduced the print yellow pages in online form.

But web users quickly became far more sophisticated and demanding as to what they expected when they searched for businesses online. It was no longer adequate to just reproduce a print ad online. People began expecting more information. They didn't want to see only what they had already seen in the phone book. After all, the Internet isn't called the information superhighway for nothing.

Now, when you go online and access a local search source like yellowbook.com, yp.com, yellowpages.com, superpages.com, etc., you will find a variety of ad products to allow your viewers the opportunity to learn more about you and your business. They can now research and make better-informed choices regarding the companies with which they will do business.

And you, the advertiser, have the opportunity to compete on whatever level of visibility you may wish, depending on what investment you are ready to make.

You can purchase banner ads that can drive traffic straight from the Internet yellow pages to your website. Banner ads and some other blocks of ad space will appear at the top and sides of the search-results pages above and around the search-results columns.

You can secure a number of positions at the beginning of the search-results listings under the appropriate heading(s). These may be referred to as *top placement* or *priority placement* listings.

Anyone clicking on your listing link will be taken to a profile page, sometimes referred to as a landing page, to provide specific information about your business's services and/or products.

An online commercial, a "commercial on demand," may be included with some programs. Ask about the availability of an online coupon with your landing pages. The obvious advantage is that you have no printing cost involved. If the customer wants to utilize the offer, they will print it and bring it to you. No printing, no mailing, no waste is involved.

Even more enhancements may be available, so check with your providers to learn what your options are. You should also be able to have a hotlink from these landing pages to your own website. Include an e-mail contact and social media links if possible.

One of the added benefits to this line of advertising is that these local search vehicles are also picked up by the major search engines and are included in the "organic" sections of their search-results pages.

MAJOR SEARCH ENGINES

Building a beautiful website with lots of bells, whistles, graphics, and e-commerce capability is only part of the picture. Webmasters can be pretty good at loading your site up with these features. But don't blindly depend on your webmaster to assure your connectivity to search engines.

Check out your website's rating on one of the free website-evaluation sites you can find online. The data you get from these services will give you some good information to help you communicate with

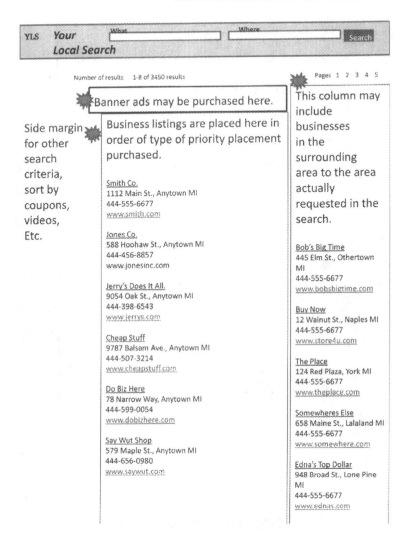

YLS **Your** What Where Search
Local Search

Number of results   1-8 of 3450 results   Pages 1 2 3 4 5

Side margin for other search criteria, sort by coupons, videos, Etc.

Banner ads may be purchased here.

Business listings are placed here in order of type of priority placement purchased.

Smith Co.
1112 Main St., Anytown MI
444-555-6677
www.smith.com

Jones Co.
588 Hoohaw St., Anytown MI
444-456-8857
www.jonesinc.com

Jerry's Does It All.
9054 Oak St., Anytown MI
444-398-6543
www.jerrys.com

Cheap Stuff
9787 Balsam Ave., Anytown MI
444-507-3214
www.cheapstuff.com

Do Biz Here
78 Narrow Way, Anytown MI
444-599-0054
www.dobizhere.com

Say Wut Shop
579 Maple St., Anytown MI
444-656-0980
www.saywut.com

This column may include businesses in the surrounding area to the area actually requested in the search.

Bob's Big Time
445 Elm St., Othertown MI
444-555-6677
www.bobsbigtime.com

Buy Now
12 Walnut St., Naples MI
444-555-6677
www.store4u.com

The Place
124 Red Plaza, York MI
444-555-6677
www.theplace.com

Somewheres Else
658 Maine St., Lalaland MI
444-555-6677
www.somewhere.com

Edna's Top Dollar
948 Broad St., Lone Pine MI
444-555-6677
www.ednas.com

your webmaster and to develop ways to increase your website's visibility.

To benefit your website's search-engine ranking, you need to address keywords and meta-tag data, business registries, and blog connections. Also, tying in to profile pages you create for your business on Facebook and other social-networking sites is helpful in raising your website's visibility.

Keep your site up to date. I had a karate-school customer whose site had not been updated for over three years! Everything mentioned on his site referred to events and subject matter that was so far out of date, it was ridiculous. The longer the time is between updates and revisions of your site's info, the less relevant your information will be to search results and the less often the search engine's spiders will crawl your pages for content.

Make sure your webmaster keeps your information fresh and relevant. In my experience, it is all too common to have a business owner tell me that they know there are changes they need to have made on their site, but their webmaster just hasn't gotten around to making them—sometimes even a year later! And it isn't always because the webmaster is Cousin Eddie who did the site "free fer nuthin'" because you are family. Even companies who build websites can be slow to update or revise your content. Many of them will charge you to make changes, but make changes as needed, even if it costs a little to do so.

One cautionary note: there are many website builders out there who show a huge amount of arrogance when they think their status as "experts" is being threatened. Having dealt with them many times, I am now of the opinion that precious few of them know as much as they should and that the wisest and most knowledgeable of them will be open to learning more, just to make sure they haven't missed anything. Check out your webmaster to see where he or she falls.

If you are your own webmaster, there is no excuse to allow your site to go stale. It makes no sense to have a website and not run it correctly.

Also be sure you consider investing in solid search-engine optimization (SEO) and consider a well-managed pay-per-click program to maximize your effectiveness. Some of the pay-per-click programs will provide the management you need so you don't have to spend the time managing it yourself. Be sure to ask about how much behind-the-scenes help, including e-mail or online account reporting, you can expect from the service you are considering.

At this writing, Google, Yahoo!, Bing, and YouTube are the most prevalent search engines on the Internet. Search-engine advertising can be very lucrative if done correctly. It can be a money hole if not done correctly. This is one area you do not want to approach ignorantly. I would guess that at least half the businesses with websites don't have a clear idea about how search engines work or how they can best utilize search-engine advertising to really cash in on their services.

The search-results pages of a search engine are the pages you see after typing in the item(s) you are searching for. There are two main sections to the search-results page. The first is the right side margin and/or top banner area. Here you will find the *sponsored links*, also called *pay-per-click* advertising or *adwords* ads. You may pay for a program that will place an ad in these spots to assure that a link to your website will appear with some degree of regularity in appropriate searches. Beware the salesperson who "guarantees" you 100 percent visibility, even here.

The rest of the page, consisting of the large left column, is called the "organic" search section. Here you will find general search results based on the keywords in the search. Search engines glean keywords from many sources. The listings of information found in this organic portion of the page are not for sale but are listed by the search engines based on algorithmic formulas by which

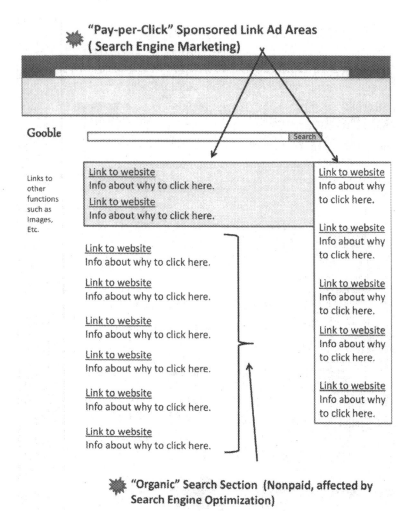

the search engines determine the relevance of the source to the keywords in the search.

If you search for "day-care centers," you may find links to sites with information on starting a day-care center of your own or on choosing a day-care center or on regulations governing the operation of day-care centers, or you may find links to day-care center websites or local search vehicles such as superpages.com, yellowbook.com, yellowpages.com, citysearch.com, or many others with listings of day-care centers in the area.

Your site may come up in this organic search section as well, but there is no guarantee that it will be there or that it will be there with any set regularity. The way to maximize the possibility of your being seen here is to make sure your site is search-engine optimized.

There are ways to register your business information with the major search engines. One free registration source is www.getlisted.org, where you will be able to enter your business information on Google, Yahoo!, Bing, Yelp, Best of the Web, and many others with which you may not be familiar. These listings, once claimed, won't guarantee your visibility online, but they will enhance your overall online visibility as the search engines check these sources for information about you.

Registering your business profile information on the search engines is a little like entering a contest or playing the lottery. If you don't enter or buy a lottery ticket, it is an assured fact that you will not win. If you do participate, you will at least have a shot at it, with varying degrees of probability for success. Likewise, if you don't list your business information online, you are less likely to appear in search results.

Businesses who crow about showing up on an online map "without doin' nuthin'" are sadly misinformed about the fact that the search engines may place skeletal information about local businesses on their maps just to make sure they are showing local results. The information, if not claimed, may be old, partial, or inaccurate, so having an unclaimed dot on a map is not the end of the story. It is just the beginning.

These free map registrations are found on Google, Yahoo!, and Bing. If you have a store or shop, make sure you list your location(s) here. At this writing, these map-locator functions are free services, so there is no reason not to avail yourself of them.

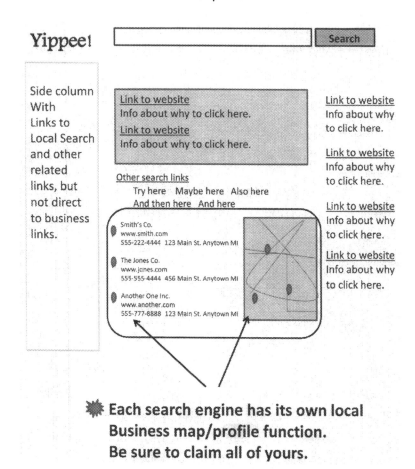

Each search engine has its own local Business map/profile function. Be sure to claim all of yours.

There are also paid services that will help you with search-engine optimization. If you don't avail yourself of and invest in these services, your online experience could be disappointing. Internet business is not a cheap and easy way to do business if you are going to do it right. You may be able to do many of the elements of SEO, but it is labor intensive. So consider investing in these services from the beginning, and increase your investment as much as possible as you grow. But do your research before you commit to make sure you are getting as much service as possible for your money.

WHAT SHOWS FROM THE ROAD: CREATIVE ADVERTISING

REFERRALS

I often hear business owners say, "All my business comes from referrals." Well, that's great. Referrals are an effective form of creative advertising. You certainly better have referrals and testimonials from people who have done business with you. Without it, you are dead in the water. In fact, every successful business started with referrals. But doing business *only* by referral is getting you a pretty slim piece of the overall market pie. You may feel that you are doing fine with nothing but word-of-mouth advertising, but it has serious limitations.

First, for the majority of potential customers in your area who could use your service or product, your word-of-mouth referrals will never be heard. In today's society it is not uncommon for people to be virtual strangers to their own neighbors. The possibility of enough interchange happening between two acquaintances to pass on the needed referral information about your business is not that high. So doing work for someone on Oak Street is no guarantee that their neighbors on Oak Street are going to hear from your customer about what a good job you did.

There is also no guarantee that those neighbors are going to flock to your customer to ask who they chose to do their work. Nor is it a given that the neighbors who hear about you are going to choose you just because their neighbor mentioned you. Offering your customer and/or the person whom they referred to you some kind of incentive will improve your chances of getting referral work.

And don't forget the impact of negative word of mouth. The longer you are in business, the more likely it is that you will come across someone who will speak badly about the job you did for them, in spite of all your efforts to correct the situation and make them happy. (You did try to make amends, didn't you?) Nonetheless, negative feedback is about ten times as strong as positive feedback. Be sure to check online review sections as well. These can work for or against you, depending on what is said there. If you feel someone has black-balled you there, see what recourse you may have with the listing source. Many times you will be able to post a response in your defense. Also, get proactive in asking your pleased customers to leave reviews to outweigh the negative one.

BUSINESS CARDS

One of the first investments some people make when starting their business is to print business cards. You may have gone online to a place like VistaPrint and received your first cards "free." Not a bad idea to begin your advertising, but remember that a business card isn't meant to really advertise your business. It is meant as a leave-behind to provide people you have met with a means of contacting you after the initial meeting.

If you leave them behind on a store counter or tacked to a bulletin board, there is no first point of contact. A card with a name and phone number really has low impact in giving someone a reason to do business with you. Not that it is a bad idea, but don't make this the mainstay of your advertising. It may bring you an occasional inquiry but not much more. And by the way, be courteous enough to ask for permission to place your cards. You may find that the policy for placement precludes your type of business. Some of those spots are for community events or nonprofit organizations only.

When designing your cards, include your business name, logo and slogan (if you have them), phone number, e-mail address, and website address. You don't want to go very much beyond these bits of information, at least on the front of the card. You want to identify yourself and give contact information here.

But consider using the back of your card as well. This is an excellent place to put bulleted information about your services/products. It will cost you more, but since information is the key to making buying decisions, using the back of the card to give reasons for doing business with you is worth considering.

CREATIVE ADVERTISING:
Find & Attract Customers

NEWSPAPERS

As with any print medium, newspaper usage has been affected by the rise of the Internet. Readership in the majority of newspaper markets is down as a result. Some newspapers have either ceased production of a paper print product altogether or have limited production to a few select editions, such as weekend or Sunday-only publications. This is more true in the larger metropolitan areas than in more rural and small-town regions. The cost of going to online publication and even the mind-set of the local population will have an effect on the rate of conversion from paper print to online versions of the newspaper.

But, like Mark Twain is said to have remarked when his obituary was accidentally published, reports of newspapers' demise are somewhat premature. In fact, although the shift to Internet media sources is increasing, print is not about to vanish from the face of the earth, regardless of what techies might say. Let's look at the strengths and limitations of print newspaper advertising.

Newspapers are a good short-term advertising medium. Most papers are read and kept for only one day. After that, they end up in the trash or recycle bin. But during that single day of usage, they are a ready source for news and information conveniently categorized in familiar sections. If you are a newspaper reader, think of which sections you gravitate to every time. Is it the sports section or the current events section or the crossword or the comic section? When you go to the barber, how many guys are sitting around reading the newspaper?

Newspapers are easily carried around and are not dependent on battery power, signal strength, or the availability of electric outlets or Wi-Fi.

If you are thinking of investing in newspaper ads, keep in mind that, in this creative advertising medium, you need to place ads based on either strong, short-term splashes (events, special sales) or on a more limited but longer-term schedule of consistent ad coverage. Plan ads with a consistent look, always including your logo and slogan.

Sale ads for Christmas, New Year's Day, President's Day, etc., should be larger ads done on a specific short-term basis. Start your ads as early as you can prior to the holiday, but balance your budget for this part of your advertising based on the size of your ad (larger is better) with the time frame during which you will be running it. If you can't go larger, at least increase the frequency with which you run the ad. Your newspaper ad rep will more than likely have special rates for holiday advertising, so be sure to ask about them when you are negotiating your ad program.

You will usually have more than one newspaper in your area. Larger cities may have one or more metropolitan dailies and a variety of community and specialty newspaper publications. Find out the coverage areas for each and consider keeping a file of each one in which you may have an interest. Call the paper to meet with one of their advertising sales reps. Develop a relationship with them. Learn how the paper sets its rates. Usually there is a cost per column inch for advertising space. The size, color, placement, and frequency with which your ad runs will all affect the price.

If you are just starting out and your budget for newspapers is very small, you may not be ready to pay for an ad in the largest coverage newspaper in your area, so consider starting with the community papers serving the areas you want to target. Many of the community and specialty papers are tabloid size, and some are nonsubscription, free publications, available either by home delivery or at convenient rack/newsstand locations. ("Free" doesn't mean free to the advertiser but free to the reader.)

Speaking of "free," you may be able to get a little free publicity if the newspapers in your area run business profiles or special-interest stories. Contact the paper and ask to speak to the business or community-interest editor. If your business story is unique, new, or in some way connects with an event of local interest, you may find that the paper will do an article on you which you can then reprint and use in other venues. This "free" exposure has limited duration, but hey, free is free. Now let's get back to our discussion of ads.

Remember that placing an ad in these papers is no guarantee that everyone in the distribution area will see your ad. Some people who receive community newspapers toss them without reading them. Many don't pick up free papers. So take the distribution figures provided by the free publications with a grain of salt. They are giving you the ideal maximum coverage figure. Make sure you understand the difference between the number of papers printed and the number actually picked up and read.

To determine how well your ads are working for you, you will have to either offer an attractive coupon or provide your customers with some other incentive to tell you they came to you because of the ad. Something like "mention this ad and get 10 percent off your order" may work. This isn't 100 percent effective, but should work well enough to help you determine how well you planned your newspaper ad program.

TELEMARKETING

There, I said it. I've mentioned the bane of every one of us who has been interrupted during dinner by someone calling to offer us a free Caribbean cruise or offering to give us a really good price break on a new set of windows. They've even tracked us down on our cell phones!

Even worse, who hasn't heard telemarketers who seem to know precisely the worst time to be calling us and are obviously reading from a script, complete with word-for-word responses to our objections. Often telemarketers either have the personality of wallpaper paste or seem to be paid by the word as they jabber on and on without ever seeming to take a breath. So we hang up on them, or tell them over and over that we aren't interested and *then* hang up on them, or we try to argue with them, all the while thinking very bad thoughts about them and their families—and maybe even telling them so. And *then* we hang up on them.

In spite of these stereotypical scenarios, there is a place for telemarketing in your ad program. The answers to many of the problems with telemarketing are in the very situations at which I poked fun.

Hire professional (or at least professional-sounding) people to man the phones. Make sure they are personable, polite, and articulate. A good command of the English language is a prerequisite. At least it is if you are in the United States. You are going to be asking your telephone sales (T-sales) force to do a very difficult job, so do all you can to prevent problems from the get-go and treat them as well as you can. Have a way to manage quality control, either by recording or listening in on the calls and making observations and suggestions to help them.

Give them a well-written script, and require that they make it their own, covering the important points of the script without requiring a word-for-word, canned presentation. Allow them to express an upbeat, positive demeanor when talking to a potential customer. It requires development, supervision, and probably a little investment in quality training to make your phone force stand out and get the job done in ways that other telemarketers will never be able to match.

TELEVISION

This technological marvel is one of the glitziest, most glamourous forms of advertising there is. And with the advent of online services like YouTube, the visual and audio impact of a good commercial can be powerful. The more of your audience's senses you can engage, the easier it is to brand your product. We remember more of what we see *and* hear than we do of what we receive through just one or the other of these two senses. If you choose to invest in television commercials, there are a few principles to bear in mind.

For most businesses, prime time on network television just isn't going to be in the budget. Not for a long time anyway, if ever. But the spots on local stations and cable stations are within the reach of many local businesses.

The next time you watch television for an evening, note when, how often, and how many local-business commercials run. Most of us don't think about whether the commercials we are seeing are for national brands and companies or for local businesses such as car dealers, stores, etc. If you see ads for local companies, this ought to show you the viability of doing ads in this medium yourself.

Production costs need to be considered, along with when and how often your ads will be shown. What channels will they play on? Who are the most likely viewers of the channel? Is there a close fit to the profile of your ideal customer? If I could use your business but I don't watch the right channel, you just *lost* my business *if* I base my decision on your commercial alone. If it airs at three in the morning you are going to miss me and a lot of others as well, even though your cost to air it at that time might be low.

Is your business name and message branded strongly enough that I will remember you after the commercial has aired? How many times have you seen a very funny or witty commercial but later you can't remember what company—or even what product—it was advertising? Think about it right now. I am sure you will come up with one or more. If you can remember the humor or the visual but you can't clearly connect it with the company running the ad, the commercial was a failure, no matter how memorable it was. Additionally, some people channel surf or use Tivo to avoid commercials regardless of how good or bad they may be.

How many times have you gotten the phone number for a business off the television commercial? Probably seldom, if ever. If you are expecting most of your phone calls or online contacts to come from TV commercials, you have a wrong expectation of what this medium is best at doing for you. You want your TV presence to be backed up by some directional advertising to make the final connection between the customer and you.

TV commercials are creative advertising. Remember what creative advertising is meant to do. First, you are attempting to build an awareness of your business and to brand your product so well that people will remember your name when they have the need. Your message is going out to a viewing audience indiscriminately, without targeting those who have an immediate interest or need. You are building top-of-mind awareness.

Second, if you are using your TV ads to announce a special offer or sale, you want to see an immediate response with droves of people showing up to take advantage of your short-term event. These are two strengths of television advertising. The weakness is in the short attention spans and memories of your audience. Repetition is the key to success.

RADIO

There are similarities among the strengths, weaknesses, and purposes of radio ads and television commercials. You might think of radio as television without pictures. I know this sounds like a duh statement, but you need to spend time thinking about it. What type of audience listens to the particular stations you are considering? When are people most likely to listen? One strong draw is morning and evening rush hour. For half an hour to an hour or so, you may have a captive audience every day from Monday through Friday. For the average person on the way to or from work, radio may be a constant companion.

If you can't budget for rush hours every weekday, consider sponsoring a program that in some way relates to your business service or products or about which you have a special interest. Even if it airs just once a week, at least you will have a solid lock on consistent exposure.

Some offices and workplaces have a radio playing as background to provide a diversion or entertainment during work. They may also play it to keep from going stir crazy in their cubicles and stabbing their coworkers with plastic forks from the kitchenette. In any case, you will want to determine which are the most popular stations for this type of listening audience and advertise there.

Another point to remember about this medium is that repetition is a necessity. You have probably heard it said that a person needs to hear or see a message a certain number of times before the message is remembered. Some say that number is three. Some say seven. In reality, there is no magic number of repetitions. The point is that *the message needs to be repeated.*

The more often you can play your ad, the better. Everyone knows about McDonald's. You probably know the location of every McDonald's within at least a five-mile radius of your home, whether you eat fast food or not. And you know that they make Big Macs and Egg McMuffins, whether you eat them or not. So why do you suppose they continually run ads on radio and television? They know the value of top-of-mind awareness. You know about McDonald's because they constantly keep their name, logo, image, and products in front of your face and in your ears by using creative advertising very effectively.

Repetition is the key. Repetition is the key. Repetition is the key. And finally, for the greatest success in television and radio advertising, repetition, along with continuity, is the key.

Be committed to investing consistently in these forms of advertising. If you choose to run ads on television or radio, your challenge will be to maintain that program for the long haul. Another strong point of this medium is in its ability to communicate short-term messages, such as short-term sales you might run for your grand opening or for Christmas or Independence Day. For those events, a short-term blitz will work very well.

BILLBOARDS

Billboards have been around in one form or another for a very long time. Even in ancient times, as in the city of Pompeii, Italy, the equivalent to billboards have been found. Business ads or, in the case of Babylonian kings, stone carvings boasting about their military success (advertising) placed along routes of travel have a long history as a basic form of creative advertising. Branding.

TOMA. ("Nebuchadnezzar, he's our man. If he can't conquer you, nobody can!")

One of the recent advances in billboard advertising is the advent of electronic billboards. Some are mechanical, with vertical slats changing the ad every few seconds. Others are digital, with the images changing more like a large television screen. In either case, this provides the opportunity for more advertisers to share the same billboard location. The billboard company can charge more businesses for the same square footage of real estate.

Ads on LED-illuminated billboards cost more than traditional billboard ads. (Go figure!) You'll have to check into the rates in your area, but a traditional board can cost, on average, anywhere from $200 to $1,800 per month and up, depending on the size, placement, and length of run of the board. The ad rate will also be influenced by the population of the area, and you may need to pay additional set-up or art fees for the development of the ad itself.

Electronic billboard ads usually last about eight seconds per viewing, but some studies show that they are about six times more effective in gaining attention than traditional boards are.

As with other forms of advertising, the more you buy, the cheaper your rates, so consider multiple billboard locations. You obviously want to choose boards in well traveled-areas and with good visibility. But don't expect more than you should from this form of advertising.

Regardless of the type of billboard you choose, keep in mind that the board's message has to be concise and catchy. Unless the people reading the sign are stuck at a red light, they won't have more than a few brief seconds to see, read, and comprehend your sign. So make the images memorable, keep the wording short and legible, and aim to include some kind of call to action.

I refer to the three indispensable things an effective billboard should have as "Honest AIB." A billboard should attract *attention,* build *interest,* and *brand* your business. This is one of the places to broadcast your strongest branding efforts. Even though most people won't have the opportunity or the presence of mind to take note of it, include your phone number and website address. This should be standard operating procedure for every ad you do in any medium.

Billboard salespeople will talk about "impressions" when touting their product. Impressions are the number of people who are calculated to pass by the billboard on a daily basis. The number of impressions will need to be very large, since the billboard's main purpose is not to directly generate leads but to build top-of-mind awareness by repeated exposure to the message over an extended period of time. So the number of impressions should not wow you into thinking the billboard is going to drive an avalanche of business to you. Remember to think practically.

How many billboards can you remember seeing right now? Can you remember the actual business being advertised? Have you ever contacted a business directly from the information you saw on the board? Do you consider billboards to be eyesores? I'm not trying to discourage you from using billboards. They can be very effective as a creative advertising tool. But I am reminding you to use them properly.

Keep in mind that if I don't drive the road along which you have your billboard, it does me no good. If I am just passing through your area, I may see your billboard and am therefore counted in your impressions, but I won't be paying much attention to your message, since it won't relate to me.

Additionally, you probably won't be able to blanket your entire area by being on every possible billboard or on every main thoroughfare. So choose wisely, and don't expect more than a billboard can deliver. Long-term branding is the strength of this medium. For those passing by your billboard, repeated long-term exposure will help to imbed your ad in their memories. Limited viewing time, eye pollution, and being passively ignored or forgotten are some of the negative factors to consider.

I'll have more on other outdoor signage later, so when you get there, remember what you read here as well, since some of these points will apply to any outdoor advertising.

INDOOR MINI ADS

Let's turn our attention now to what I call "mini ads." These are like teeny-weeny little billboards that show up in the darnedest places. Have you ever been in a restaurant and had a paper placemat that had about twenty or so small ads printed all around the edge? How about sitting at a table with a top that has been laminated with ads? Or picking up a city map that is bordered all around with little ads for local businesses? How about those stickies that you find on the top of pizza boxes, phone-book covers, newspapers, etc.?

If you decide to do this type of advertising, make sure you are aware that the primary purpose of these little ads is just to place your name in front of people—to build top-of-mind awareness. Some may include a call-to-action offer.

If you are expecting a large increase in business through this type of advertising, you are setting an improper expectation and you will most likely be disappointed. Your audience is small compared to the total population, your presence is not at all targeted to any particular group, and if you don't make this an ongoing, long-term campaign, you'll be diminishing the impact of your program.

On the other hand, if cheap is your main criterion for your choice of mini ads, the investment in most of these forms will be small. So consider the cost and determine if it is reasonable enough to be used for its intended purpose.

I remember seeing a unique device built into a wall clock in a small rural restaurant/diner. Beside the clock was a nifty little flip chart that would show an ad for a few seconds, and then the top would flip down to show another ad, and so on. This is a pretty good idea as long as you want to know what time it is or if the service is slow. Takes your mind off the waiting while Flo is in the back trying to get Chester to grill your cheese sandwich a little faster.

If the mini-sign product is low cost, it is not necessarily a bad investment; nor is it necessarily a good investment. Just remember that you are limiting your exposure to only those people who visit that restaurant or who pick up that city map or whatever. Low cost is not the reason you want to invest in the program. Although not a bad idea, these types of advertisements should not be the major part of your overall campaign. They should be augments to a more far-reaching and comprehensive ad program.

OUTDOOR SIGNS

We just covered indoor "mini signs." Now let's go back outside. I covered billboards in a previous section, and it would be a good idea to read that section again after you finish this one, since there will be some points both of these categories will have in common. Here I am concentrating on the many smaller visibility opportunities for outdoor advertising.

These tools will differ from billboards in the level of visibility, investment, and scope. Their reach is far more localized than that provided by billboards, and the cost is lower.

Yard signs. We have all seen them. Roofers and other contractors like them a lot. While working on a home or once they finish a job, they proudly proclaim their handiwork by sticking their sign in the front yards of their customers.

It's better than word of mouth, since without the prompting of the sign, it isn't as likely that the neighbors up and down the street will take the initiative to ask who did the job. This way, they will know without asking, whether they wanted to know or not.

I know that these signs work because contractors tell me they do. Be sure to include your phone number along with the business name in VERY LARGE NUMBERS AND LETTERS. Make *everything* readable from a good distance. The biggest mistake made with these signs is having too much text and writing it in too small a font. Here's your sign: minimum text; maximum readability.

Contractor yard signs have a limited life span. They may stay for a few weeks, but eventually either the contractor comes by to take it down to reuse or the customer gets tired of it and removes it.

Remember that in most cases I will see the sign while I am driving. And just as it is with billboards, I can't usually write down a number, or even a business name, while I am driving. So although you may get a few jobs from yard signs, your main purpose in planting these signs is still building top-of-mind awareness. And make sure that you retrieve them for reuse after they have been in the yard for an agreed-upon length of time. I have heard that sometimes evil competitors will swipe them too. Something to think about.

Roadside bench or bus stop signs are another way to build name recognition when placed on well-traveled streets or roads. You will also see them in rural settings on the sides of school bus stop shelters. Even barn-side painted signs may be included here, although you might want to think of barn signs as falling more into the billboard category.

Keep in mind that, whichever of these venues you use, you have to maintain it for the long term. How many of these signs did you probably drive by today? Can you remember anything specific about them right now? Your answer demonstrates why you need to run these campaigns for the long term. Keep in mind that, even with longevity, your sign may be ignored by many.

MOBILE ADVERTISING

Make your car or truck a traveling billboard by having, at a minimum, your business name, web address, and phone number placed on its sides. Wherever you are parked, and even when in motion, you will be proclaiming your business to whoever sees you. Once in a while, you may get a new offer for work while on a current job site. You may find that someone riding in a lane beside you may see your name and call you on your cell while you are driving.

Vehicle advertising takes various forms. Some start-up businesses may invest in simple magnetic signs on their doors. These have the advantage of being easily removed for transfer from one vehicle to another or for removal when you are using the car off duty and are not interested in having your car identified as a business vehicle.

Another low-key type of vehicle advertising is window-graphic signage. Here the graphics are most often applied to window space on the sides and rear windows. In both magnetic and window graphics, you will want to make sure your signage is legible (avoid fancy curlicue fonts) and large enough to be easily readable. Remember that in most cases, your audience only has a few seconds to see and understand your message. Also keep in mind that this should not be your main source getting leads. If I am driving, I don't usually have the freedom to easily jot down your contact information.

Some companies use vehicle "skins," which make the entire body of the car or truck into a billboard. If you use this form of vehicle advertising, be sure to make maximum use of the medium, including color, logos, and ad text. You want the skin to be eye-catching and to communicate clearly who you are, what you do, and how you want people to contact you.

Other versions of this medium include portable billboard trucks and trucks with mounted objects (such as a giant Red Bull can in the truck bed) that just drive around all day over a given area.

This is especially effective when done to announce a new product or a business opening or event. The more eye-catching the display, the better. This will work best if done as a short-term campaign, since even the most creative spectacle will lose its punch after the initial few impacts. After that, it gets a little ho-hum. As the Queen of England might say, "We are no longer amused."

Businesses with more modest rooftop displays don't fall into the ho-hum category, since these examples of signage are used for company branding. NAPA, a national auto parts company, uses (at this writing anyway) a large NAPA ball cap on many of their delivery trucks. Pizza shops may have a taxi-type lit sign. These examples of mobile advertising are better as long-term, consistent forms of company identification. Who doesn't want to know when the pizza delivery guy arrives? Late. With the wrong pizza. With half the toppings stuck to the roof of the cardboard box. At least you'll know it was the right pizza shop. The car had the lit sign on top.

DIRECT MAIL

This medium provides many ways to select coverage. You can choose to focus on particular geographic areas, such as zip code areas, either hitting the same areas with a set regularity or hitting different areas on a rotation basis.

Envelopes containing flyers and coupons from various businesses are one example of nonspecific advertising. In most cases, you will simply choose the areas or zip codes you want to cover, and your flyer, along with those of any number of other businesses, including some of your competitors, will go into the envelopes for that area. In most cases, the only targeting available is choosing the zip codes to which you wish to mail.

If you don't mind having your flyer in the same envelope with others, some of whom are your competitors, this might be a way to go. If your coupon or flyer is in the envelope with a competitor's, the consumer will most likely choose whichever of you seems to be making the best offer, since they will have the easy opportunity of comparing your flyers side by side.

On the other hand, consider the advantages to the more expensive direct-mail approach of sending out a single-piece mailer. Often these will be large postcards or unique flyers. The better the quality, the better it is for your company's image, so even though your cost will be higher, the advantage to your professional reputation is obvious.

Along with options in color, size, postage class, and frequency of mailing, another important consideration is to make sure the mailing list your direct-mail vendor uses is as current as possible. A cheap list may be two or more years old. Every mailer you send out to an old address will be a total waste. For every mailer either thrown out by an unintended recipient or marked "Return to Sender," your "cheap" rate goes up. So, although you will pay more for the most current list possible, the investment is worth it to limit wasted postage. Most lower-cost mailing companies use older lists.

Depending on the vendor, you may be able to use extensive demographic breakdowns to target, for example, families with children and with incomes over $75,000 per year. This demographic tuning will cost more than the zip code blanketing approach, but you will be able to reach a more specific group. To make the best use of the more targeted approach, be sure to define your target market. What does your ideal customer look like in regard to income, home ownership, family size, possessions, etc.? These criteria will help you build your list.

Also, if you already have your own list of previous customers, consider merging them into your mailing, but don't limit your mailing to current or past customers. Otherwise, you will be preaching to the choir rather than looking to expand your customer base.

The less demographically tuned approach, mailing to specific zip code areas, may not seem as focused on any particular group of consumers, but that isn't necessarily as bad as it may sound. The strength here is that within any given area, there will be people who may need your business at some time. Do you clean carpets? Are you concerned about a part of the zip code–based mailings you send out ending up in the hands of apartment dwellers? That's true. But which of those apartment dwellers will, sometime in the next year or so, turn into home buyers who may then need their carpets cleaned? Making your name known *ahead* of the time of need is part of the task of building top-of-mind awareness.

The advantage to using the more targeted demographic program is that you aren't wasting production costs and postage sending information to people who are unlikely, at least right now, to use your services. Don't expect to hit the nail squarely on the head even with this focusing capability. In most cases, you still won't be able to detect who in the demographic has an immediate interest or need for you. One of the strengths of direct mail is its ability to create and build top-of-mind awareness. Repeat your mailings on some type of schedule for the best results. Whether spring, summer, winter, fall, or back-to-school, Christmas, Easter, or the Fourth of July, plan your mailings to maximize your exposure during your best sales times.

Another strength of direct mail is its immediate call to action. I strongly recommend that you use your mail piece to make a very attractive offer to get the recipient to act now. Offer a good coupon, present a buy-one-get-one (BOGO) deal, have some kind of gadget giveaway for anyone who presents the mailer to you, etc.

Make sure your offer is strong enough to make it worth the customer's effort. I remember a restaurant whose coupon offered a "Free Can of Pop with Any Meal." Okay, Mr. Moneybags-Restaurant-Owner, are you sure you can swing an offer so generous? I would have expected an offer more like "Buy One Entrée at Regular Price and Get a Second Entrée of Equal or Lesser Value Free" (or at least at half price).

When developing your offer, make sure that the duration of the offer is clearly stated, and include any other disclaimers, terms, and conditions that need to apply to keep the program from costing you more than you anticipated. This is true for any coupon you develop, regardless of where you place it. The main rule to apply to any coupon offer is: *make the offer strong enough that it almost hurts to give the offer.* The word to emphasize is "almost." Think like a customer. If you have two offers for a product or service, which would you be most likely to use, an offer for 10 percent off or half price?

Plan your direct-mail campaign to provide the most targeted coverage you can, and do it on some kind of regular basis. A low-percentage return on this form of advertising is to be expected, with 2 percent being fairly average. The response will vary according to the type of business. A pizza mailer will outperform a home builder's flyer in regard to the number of responses. Based on the differences in their products, both will be worth doing, since the home builder will more easily see a good return on his investment with far fewer leads and the pizza shop owner will receive many more responses and get a good return on his investment as well.

Unless your mailer is related to a particular upcoming event or is otherwise time sensitive, doing the mailer one time is probably a waste of effort. Determine how often you can afford to do the mailer over a maximum length of time.

There is really no foolproof way to keep your direct mail from being considered junk mail by the majority of recipients. So don't be disappointed if your beautiful, well-written, "Best Offer Ever" flyer doesn't bring you a huge influx of leads. It should, however, in the long run, more than pay for itself with even a 1 or 2 percent level of response.

SOCIAL MEDIA

With the advent of Facebook, Twitter, Linked In, and other forms of online social posting sites, the opportunities to network and provide exposure for your business have increased. Additionally, by providing inbound links from these sites to your website, you will be increasing your site's ranking and visibility with search engines. Other ways to keep your visibility strong in social media is to be sure you include as much company info as you can. Your logo, slogan, specific brand language, related keywords, and video footage/commercials all should be available to the viewers.

Keep in mind that some people use social media and some do not. For those who are active in this area, the tendency is to think that everyone else is going that way too. The view that everyone is on Facebook is misleading. If I am on the site, and all my friends are on the site, and they are directing their friends and contacts to the site (and so on and so on), I can be prone to feel that "everyone" is not only aware of it but is also using it. This just isn't the case. I feel a sense of futility in saying this, knowing that the social media activists won't want to admit that what I say is true.

I spoke to a local chamber of commerce director who is *not* a proponent of these media. In fact, she feels that these vehicles are too faddish. She hopes that they will just go away. I'm not sure that will ever happen, but we have all heard the cautionary tales about people ending up with the wrong information falling into the hands of unscrupulous people because of an unguarded online connection or unwise comment linked to a company through social media sources. Problems like this have tended to make some businesspeople skittish about using social media.

Use care and discretion in building your company's online image on social media sites. Keep all personal information off the social media profiles for the business unless you feel it will only be helpful to the company's image, and never share anything on the business site that is not fully professional or that may be used in any hurtful way.

Encourage visitors to your social media page to visit the company's website and provide a back link to the site.

I am going to include blogs and participation in online forums under this point. The term *blog* is short for "web log" and simply means an online site where you can enter anything from news items to your own commentary on any subject to an online posting location. For your business I recommend that you concentrate on those two uses: news announcements and commentary/ information.

Blogs are a free means of making information available to whomever you wish online. It provides you with an outlet to disseminate information about your business, your expertise, helpful knowledge for your potential customers, developments in your business or industry, or whatever else you want to use it for. Keep the content relevant, and don't confuse the business use of your blog with personal information. In this way you begin to establish yourself as an authority in your area of business.

Additionally, back linking your blog to your website is another way to enhance your search-engine visibility, especially when you tag the keywords you use in each entry. Relevant inbound links to your site are always desirable. If this is Greek to you, either find out more about it online or from a trusted and knowledgeable resource person (not just Cousin Eddie).

Online forums are set up by subject, and you'll find them discussing anything you can imagine. Find forums that relate to your industry or business, and get a feel for the type and quality of discussions you find there. When you feel comfortable with the quality of the conversations found there, jump in by adding comments of your own.

If you are interested in this type of communication and you feel that you can contribute to the content, you will begin to establish your credibility to a far-reaching audience. Make sure, however, that you have a decent grasp of grammar and spelling so you don't end up sounding uneducated and therefore untrustworthy. If you aren't very good at spelling and grammar, consider having a ghostwriter who can translate your thoughts into good form.

E-MAIL ADVERTISING

Do you know what spam is? Ever get any in your e-mail? Have you ever gotten advice telling you not to open spam due to computer viruses that may be lurking there? If you are online at all, I know you have.

For these reasons, e-mail advertising is best at reaching current contacts or contacts you may have solicited through sign-up offers. In any case, your best bet at gaining the attention of anyone online through e-mail will be when the recipients already know about you and are more likely to want to see what you are sending.

Make your e-mail worth reading. This is not the time to just get folksy or to bore the readers with newsletter info of interest to you and your company but not really of much use or interest to your e-mail recipients. Provide useful information or a special offer to those who take the time to open your e-mail.

But be ready for many of the recipients to send your message, unopened, to trash. That's what I do. Do I risk missing some special offer? Yes, but I'm not convinced that opening any of the offers would be worth my time or risk.

I'm not saying don't do it, but be aware first of all that this method of advertising is primarily meant to maintain existing customers. Your gain in new contacts will be minimal.

It is certainly not the means you want to use if your purpose is to reach the maximum number of new leads. Use e-mail advertising as an adjunct to the other means you are using to build your client base.

MAGAZINES

One advantage of doing magazine advertising is that you can find magazines on virtually any subject. In many cases, if your business caters to a certain type of reader with a particular interest in your product or service, you can target them by advertising in the magazine(s) they are most likely to read. If you sell hearing aids, you'll want to consider placing ads in magazines read by senior citizens. If you deal in car-care items, advertise in car magazines.

The more popular the publication, the greater the price for advertising in it. And remember the back section of some magazines where you might be able to place a small classified ad. The trade-off here is that although you will pay much less for these ads, they are overlooked by many readers. The higher-priced full-page ads in the main body of the magazine will give you a much higher top-of-mind awareness than the little classifieds. So set your expectations accordingly.

Do your research to find out what special-interest magazines are available. You'll be surprised at how many and how varied magazine publications there are. Keep in mind that everyone with the special interest will not be a subscriber or read or even be aware of the magazine. Nonetheless, as a means of reaching a unique audience, this is not a bad way to go.

MOVIE THEATER ADVERTISING

"Let's go out to the lobby; let's go out to the lobby; let's go out to the lobby, and get ourselves a treat!" Along with those little ditties that play on the movie screen before the previews, you'll find advertisers floating slides or video commercials in front of us. Usually, the ad company that does these ads will run their own ads onscreen with information about how many people go to the movies every year and are therefore bound to see your ad.

If you go to the movies and you have seen the pre-movie ads, how many do you recall right now? Did you make a decision to visit a particular dentist or to take your car for service to an auto shop based on the movie theater ad?

Maybe so, but probably not. Is it a mistake to invest in movie theater ads? Not as long as you realize that the strength of these ads is in branding your business. Unless you make a very strong offer to entice the audience to remember and contact you after the two-hour blockbuster superhero movie, don't expect a huge influx of customers from this form of advertising. Use it to build your top-of-mind awareness and your branding. You can attempt to track your movie theater ad response by tacking on an offer such as "Mention that you saw this ad and get ..."

This is the place for flash, glitz, and glamour. Make 'em laugh. Be as memorable as you can be. But don't make this the foundation of your ad program. It is a good adjunct to other media. If you have done a good job with a video commercial prepared for television, consider using it on the theater screen as well, and vice versa.

PROMOTIONAL PRODUCTS

Pens, pencils, mugs, rulers, Band-Aid holders, envelope slitter-opener thingamabobs, computer memory sticks, etc., with a company logo attached are all examples of promotional products. Sometimes they may be referred to as "chotchkies."

No, I'm not talking about the Scott Baio character who first appeared on the old TV show *Happy Days* and who then went on in a spinoff show, as in *Joanie Loves Chachi*. Sounds like, but not the same.

Chotchkies, derived from a Yiddish word for a little useless knickknack, doesn't really describe these objects well enough, since they do have uses. They have two actually. Whatever the gadget is, it has a primary function as the gadget itself. When you attach your business info/logo to it, it gains a second function: advertising for you.

Promotional products are any of those freebies you pick up at exhibits, state fair booths, business expos, and other places where businesses are trying to give you a little something to remember them by. It is usually either useful or interesting enough for you to want to pick it up and keep it. That's why you'll always find a business's name on it somewhere prominently displayed.

I once worked at a place where we had a dandy little chotchkie. It was a little plastic clip that sat on a desktop and could hold a piece of paper upright so it could be read as you typed. Another similar gadget attaches to your computer monitor to hold a paper for the same reason. Our little doodad was a hit with most people anyway. The name of the organization I represented was emblazoned on the front of it so that whether you were using the device to hold a memo, a sign, or something to be typed, the name of my organization was staring you in the face every time you looked at it.

Promotional items are popular and come in a wide variety of objects and prices, so do some research before investing in these. Try to stand out by choosing something a little out of the ordinary if you can. After all, a person only needs so many brightly colored pens. But if pens are what you go for and you can afford them, make liberal use of them.

More high-end items, such as sticky drives and WOW cards, are available as well. These are especially attractive to businesses dealing with upper-income-level consumers or business-to-business sales. These promotional items provide more detailed information about your company than most other items that only carry a logo and/or slogan. They also cost more.

Remember that these items are not meant to do the whole job of bringing you customers. This is creative advertising, so branding and name recognition are the strong suits of most promotional items.

EXHIBIT BOOTHS

You will find many opportunities to show off your business by placing a booth at trade shows, community festivals, business expos, sporting events, or fairs, to name a few. Check back to the section on promotional items for information on stocking your exhibit with advertising trinkets.

If you can't have personnel attending the booth at all times, you probably shouldn't waste your time having the booth at all. Think about it. When you go to an exhibition and go by an empty booth, what signal does it send you? How much time do you spend visiting that booth? Just having space at an event isn't enough to make this an effective advertising opportunity. Avoid like the plague the tendency to have a booth just because "that's what we've always done."

When you are manning an exhibition booth and you have promotional items displayed, get proactive and *hand* them out. I've done plenty of exhibit booth duty in my time, and believe me, beyond the more personal contact and higher level of interest you create, it is just more fun to attempt a little interaction with the people going by. You will generate a lot more leads by being a little more aggressive at your booth. Have fun and be friendly. Show an interest in the people you get to talk to, but don't be overly pushy.

There is nothing more pathetic than going by a booth where the attendants are just sitting there talking to each other or trying to look past everyone, almost as if they were hoping no one would approach them. They make the old Maytag repairman look like Dale Carnegie by comparison. Okay, so I know I am dating myself with some of these comparisons. See, the Maytag repairman was supposed to be very lonely because his brand never seemed to break down, so he never got to do anything. On the other hand, Dale Carnegie … Oh, never mind. Google it.

ORGANIZATIONAL MEMBERSHIPS

If you are a member of a guild, trade association, small local business owners' group, or some other professional organization, check into the advertising opportunities the organization may offer. This could be anything from free business listing information on the group's website to free or low-cost advertising in a newsletter or other publication.

You may also get membership discounts for advertising programs the organization has in other media. Additionally, holding membership in a recognized association lends credence to your business due to the professional acknowledgement you receive.

LOCAL COMMUNITY ONLINE ADVERTISING

Chambers of commerce and other community-related websites are another source of exposure for your business. I recommend becoming a member of your local chamber. Yes, I know that sometimes these groups can be clique-ish mutual admiration societies, but the opportunities to increase your visibility and to network with other local businesspeople could be very helpful to your business's growth.

Consider taking advantage of everything they have to offer in regard to advertising, whether it is in the organization's newsletter or some other means of outreach. Who knows? Maybe you can change that country-club reputation by your participation. A group that simply rotates the officers within a small elitist crowd needs an infusion of new blood.

COMMUNITY INVOLVEMENT/FUND RAISING

When I ask a business about their current advertising, I know that there is trouble when they tell me a major part of what they do is community involvement. Whether the medium is yearbook ads, infield ballpark fence ads, score boards, or fund-raiser participation, there is trouble in River City if these are the main means of outreach.

It is good public relations, it is certainly laudable, and if the situation seems right, it might be okay to do it. But again, as with many of these peripheral media, never make the mistake of substituting the staples of your advertising diet for the tantalizing little delicacies that give additional flavor to your program. Once again, this is an area that should be looked upon as an augment to your meat-and-potatoes advertising.

If you contribute money or materials to a fund-raising event, my advice is to do so only if you truly want to contribute to the cause. Let's face it. If your intentions were totally altruistic, you wouldn't concern yourself with promotion of your business name. You would remain anonymous while making your contribution. So dive in. Be committed. Be involved. But don't consider community involvement as your primary means to promote your business. In this regard, be selfless. The benefit to your business will come one way or another without forcing it.

ODDS 'N ENDS

The stream of creative advertising means and methods is never ending. I could go on into many other areas, such as listing your products on eBay, inserts sent out with customer billings or invoices, cooperative efforts such as cross-promotion with other businesses, and more. I have tried to cover the major forms as much as possible. For any additional types of creative advertising, the principles and guidelines I have shared will apply to those as well.

Since I am bound to miss some along the way, bear with me and learn what to look for and what to expect from any others by applying the guidelines from the ones I have included.

If you now have a clear grasp of the characteristics and principles governing both directional and creative advertising, you will be able to build your own advertising program in a much more efficient, intelligent, and cost-effective way.

SUPERCHARGING YOUR WEBSITE

WHERE DOES YOUR WEBSITE FIT?

You now know the differences between directional and creative advertising and which media fit in which category, but you may be wondering in which of these categories your website belongs. Actually, it doesn't belong in either category. Forget what you may have heard or read about your website being an ad for your business. Pay attention to this and you'll see why I strongly disagree about considering your site as another ad.

Your advertising media are the roads that lead to a destination. The destination is your business. Your website is not an advertising medium. It is your representative. Just as your office, your store, or your presence on the worksite do, your website provides the complete picture of what you and your business are. Your pay-per-click adwords ads, your online banner ads, and your appearances in organic search results are the ads meant to drive traffic to your site. If you conduct e-commerce on your site, it is just as much your store as a brick-and-mortar establishment is.

In fact, the trend in business is to direct all advertising toward driving traffic to your website. This means more than just making sure your website address is included in your ads. It means including language meant to invite seekers to visit your site. Wording like "For more information, visit our website at …," "See our website for special offers," or "Order yours today at www.mybusinesshere .com." This is why it is so crucial not only to *have* a website but to make sure it is easily found and accessible.

I want to throw my hands up in despair when I ask a business owner if they are found on the Internet and they say, "Sure." Then they proceed to type in their domain name, and when it pops up, they step back and say, "Looky there. There I am!" This is totally missing the point. If that website doesn't appear to people who are looking for the business in a *general search* for the type of business, the site is, for all practical purposes, invisible and therefore not much good.

HOW VISIBLE ARE YOU?

There is a major difference between having a website and having it actually serve as a means to promote your business. There are many ways to develop a website. Some are free. Some are very low cost. Some are do-it-yourself programs. Some are built for you by companies who specialize in building websites. Any of these methods can work for you if you approach them knowledgeably.

Whichever type you choose, there are very important factors you need to keep in mind. A free template website may seem to be better than nothing, but remember that this site, even if it is a single-page site, represents you to the world. If you want your image to look chintzy, go for the cheap, free site. Personally, I don't think you want to start out that way. But it is your choice. Your website should reflect a high degree of professionalism. But even the best-looking site, with all sorts of bells and whistles, graphics, flash programs, and audio, won't do much good if you don't cover a few other important bases.

Having a website without including search-engine optimization is like buying a car without buying any gas to run it. It can sit in the garage and look pretty, but it isn't going to take you anywhere. Optimization entails building your site with the appropriate structure and information to have it noticed by the search engines.

I don't build websites. I can't tell you how to build one, but I can give you a few tips to make sure you build your site to help your optimization.

First, realize that the search engines are not impressed with the great artwork you have on your home page. In fact, to the search engines, your photos, PDFs, and flash programs are just big empty spots. To be noticed they must be properly tagged. Search engines are only interested in the content and wording on your site.

Go to a website right now. Place your cursor in some clean spot on the page. Not on a picture, and not on text. Right-click in this area. If you have placed your cursor in the correct area, you will see a menu pop up. Somewhere toward the middle of this menu you should find something called "View Source" or "View Page Source." If you don't, move your cursor to another clear area on the page until you do. Click on "View Source" and you will have a behind-the-scenes look at the website.

Now look for a section called "title." You will often see nothing more than the name of a business here. This is not so good. The title line should contain only two or three items, the least important of which is the business name. There should be a subject modifier to describe what the site is about, like "Heating & Cooling Service" and a geo-modifier, such as "Central Ohio" or "Chicago, Illinois," to specify the area in which my store or office is located or where I provide my services.

If your business is not limited to a geographic area by way of store location (such as with an e-commerce site), protected territory, or travel constraints, you don't need a geo-modifier. But ordinarily you will want to tell the search engines where you are located so they know to include you in searches for your area.

The only time the company name is of any relevance here is if the subject of the site is part of the name, such as "Tom's Auto Repair." The word "Tom's" has less relevance, but the rest of the name, "Auto Repair," does relate to the site's subject. If the business name is "The Smith Company," there is nothing in the name that indicates the nature of the business, and it does not help to include the business name at all on the title line. The only exception to this guideline is when the business name is actually included in the search request. In other words, if I have done enough creative advertising to make my brand a sought-after name, then I will want to include it.

Therefore, the business name, if included at all on the title meta tag, is the third most important thing to have on the title meta tag. This title tag should be no longer than about sixty-five characters, including spaces and dashes or commas. I recommend that you do not include the business name here unless you can fit it in after the subject and geo-modifier wording. If it doesn't fit, after putting in your main subject search word and geo-modifier, don't include the name. There are other places where it will be included.

In the organic section of search-results pages (the main left column), the blue underlined text of each search result contains the title line info. If you look carefully at these lines, you will see that certain words in the line are bolded. These are the words that were used in your search. The bold words are the only ones the search engine has keyed for relevance to the search. Those are the words the searcher placed in the search bar, and that is what the search engines want to find there.

Example of an incorrect title meta tag:

```
<title>Home - Carefree Lawn Care Beautiful lawns Don't
happen by Themselves</title>
```

Example of a properly built title meta tag:

```
<title> Auto Insurance | Newark OH | Reinhard &
Daughter Insurance</title>
```

Next, on that behind-the-scenes page, look for a section called "meta tag description." This section contains a short, thumbnail sketch of the information on the site. This is the place to include the business name, a geo-modifier, and a brief description of who you are and what you do.

Go back to the search-results page on your search engine. The black text under the blue underlined links should be the description meta tag. It should be concise, and should start with the business name. It should then tell where you are located and what you do. As with the title meta tag, if your business has no need to focus on a geographic area, leave out the geo information.

Example of a properly written description meta tag:

```
<meta name="description" content="Mid-State Industrial
Services, Inc., based in the Marion, Ohio area, has
been providing quality industrial contracting with
over 35 years experience.">
```

Spiders is one term for search engines' programs that are constantly crawling the web to find pertinent sites to enter into search results. If you want these critters to find your site, you need to provide easy access by helping to make your information simple for them to locate.

Another area on that behind-the-scenes page is "meta-keywords." This section should include any wording you think a potential customer might use to look you up. For a dog groomer, you might want to include dog grooming, dog groomer, dog groomers, pet grooming, pet groomer, pet groomers, cat grooming, cat groomer, cat groomers, dog-nail trimming, dog-nail trimmer, dog-nail trimmers, flea treatment, tick treatment, etc. Include pertinent geo-modifier keywords, such as "Dallas Texas, Amarillo Texas, Austin Texas."

Note that keywords are not just single words. Think of keywords as *word units.* Also, as in my example, realize that singular and plural forms of the same keyword unit are considered entirely separate keywords. So don't forget to include both singular and plural forms.

Please note: Google no longer references the keyword meta tag section, so even though it is a good idea to include keywords here, it is much more important to *use the keywords in the actual text on the page.* Try to utilize the relevant keyword units on the page anywhere from three to seven times, depending on the overall page text. Use them in sentences, bullet-pointed lists, summary paragraphs, etc.

Now that you have an idea of some of the most important onsite optimization principles for a website page, I want you to pay close attention to this: *each page* of your site should have its own title meta tag and its own description meta tag specifically geared to the content of that page. This is why your multipage site should be built around profit centers rather than extraneous information. Save the About Us, History, or Gallery pages for last, if at all. Most searchers won't primarily be looking you up to see where you went to school or how many times your business has moved or what your family looks like. Save those things for your social media areas or for additional web pages after building your profit center pages.

What I mean is, don't waste your pages on History, About Us, etc., when you could have one page for landscaping, one for snow plowing, one for lawn maintenance, one for patio building, etc. If you want a page for photos, a gallery of your work, fine, but keep in mind that most people won't be searching for that as their first priority.

The reason for building profit center–related pages is that, if you have done your meta tags properly for each page, searchers will land on the page they are actually most interested in rather than on your Home page. If all the traffic is being directed to your Home page, it means that your site visitors have to click again to get to what they are really after. You don't want this. The fewer times visitors have to click to get to what they want, the better.

Although onsite optimization is only about 15 to 17 percent of total optimization, the effect of doing this part right can go a long way toward moving your site from invisibility to visibility. If you are doing your 15 to 17 percent correctly and the majority of your competitors are not, your site may surpass theirs in visibility. And don't expect the changes to be an overnight success. It commonly takes three to six months for a site to gain in positioning and ranking with any optimization that is done.

There is much more to search-engine optimization (SEO), including blogging, social media, online video, news releases, back linking, indexing, etc., so it is worth the time and effort to either learn how to optimize your site or to pay someone who is proficient at it to do it for you. This is not an unnecessary frill. It is a necessity. Start with internal (onsite) optimization as I have laid it out here and then, as you can, expand into some of the other external things you can do.

One other thing: go to www.getlisted.org and claim your business listings with over a dozen online business listing sources. It doesn't matter whether you have heard of them or not. These listing resources are part of what I call the "horizontal networking" available to you.

When you pay for a professionally created site, the initial cost of building your site may be very low. There is a reason for this. You are only getting the site itself. Remember the car-in-the-garage analogy? The website-building fee and the hosting fee are only the beginning. Unless you want your site to be a secret, only for an initiated crowd, you will need to either pay for search-engine optimization or attempt to do it yourself. This is where a greater portion of your website cost may go.

So if you think that your website was a real steal because it was so cheap, think again. You get what you pay for. Having Cousin Eddie build your site "free fer nuthin'" will get you just what you deserve: nuthin'. Advertising your website the right way will require a reasonable expenditure.

A final important area I want you to consider when paying someone to build your website deals with the policy the builder has regarding changes to your site. You should make periodic changes to your site to keep your website's visibility score as high as possible. If the spiders attempt to crawl your site but see that there hasn't been any new information added for quite some time, they will, in a sense, get bored with it and begin going elsewhere to find fresher relevant content to throw into the search results. You don't have to rebuild or get drastic, but every couple of months or so, add or rework some of your information.

When hiring your website builder, ask about their policy and fees regarding any content changes to your site. When you want to make changes, is there a charge for making them? Do they allow a certain number of changes to be made for free, after which you will be charged? If they allow self-editing, how will you know whether the changes will hurt or help your website's search-engine ranking?

My purpose in giving you this information is not to provide everything you need to know about building, optimizing, and maintaining your website. I simply want to open your eyes to aspects of website advertising about which you need to be aware. I have seen too many small businesses making mistakes in online advertising and carrying on in blissful ignorance of just how useless their invisible website is and how wasteful their bargain-basement approach to the Internet really is. Don't be one of them.

CREATING DYNAMITE ADS

AD-BUILDING TIPS

I am not going to go into a lot of detail about things like the value of color in ads, because it seems to be too common-sense to belabor the fact that a full-color ad draws more attention and looks better and is more professional than one that is black and white or, in the case of yellow pages, black on yellow. If you don't get this, do a little research and you'll find all the facts to prove it.

The same goes for ad size. Generally speaking, the bigger the ad the better. If I were *giving away* full-page ads in a magazine, newspaper, or phone book, there is not a sensible businessperson in the world that would turn it down. The reason? Duh! The larger the ad, the more attention it draws. This, my friend, is also common sense. It is a proven, demonstrable fact, just like the color discussion above. It is a perfectly understood fact until ... an advertising representative tries to sell *you* a larger ad. Then, all of a sudden, none of that seemingly applies. Reason tends to go right out the window when it may mean investing more in your ads to get an increased market share from your advertising program.

At that point common sense takes a long hike. I've seen it many times in my illustrious career. These facts—these commonsense truths—suddenly become irrelevant and unnecessary. Somehow it becomes more likely and more obvious that the scheming, money-grabbing ad salesperson just wants a higher commission by selling you a larger ad for no good reason whatsoever.

I'm not saying that every ad you do has to be large and in color. Certainly, whatever you decide will have to fit your budget. But if your veteran competitors have large, color ads and you are running a very small, colorless ad, don't blame your ad salesman if you don't generate as many sales from your ad as the other guy. It just ain't gonna happen.

I have had some business owners tell me that they don't want a large ad because they feel that potential customers avoid the larger ads on the assumption that a company that has to pay for a large ad must charge more for their services. You go right on thinking that, my friend. Your competitor with the large ad will appreciate it too. The fewer serious competitors they have, the better.

So that's all I have to say about size and color. Make use of them or don't. But don't get silly and say that they don't matter. No one will believe you, especially your ad representative, and it won't change the facts.

AD CONTENT

Ad placement is important, of course, but what you say in an ad will dictate the type of response you get. In most cases, save the full-sentence storytelling for your website, where people expect to get the whole picture of your business: who you are, how you started, your mission statement, all the products or services you sell, and so on.

Content is king! The key to your ad building is to have a clear message that will persuade a potential customer to do business with you. This may sound trite, but simply ask yourself, *Why would anyone want to do business with me rather than the next guy?* If you can answer that question, you will begin to have an idea about how to build an effective advertising message. If you can't clearly answer the question, what in the world are you in business for? In attempting to help a new business develop an ad campaign, I have asked the owner, "Why should someone do business with you rather than someone else?" and sometimes I have gotten a blank stare.

In an earlier section on reasons for business failure, I discussed the need to have more than making money as your motivation. The blank stare often comes when money is the only reason you can think of for being in business. That will also make it difficult to come up with an effective ad. If you don't know what sets you apart, makes you better, or provides a clearer benefit to your potential customers, how are you going to convince them to contact you?

So make sure you take the time to develop a clear picture of the advantages someone would have in doing business with you. Once you can express that reason, you are on your way to building an effective ad campaign.

Here are some key elements to include in virtually every ad you build. First, determine whether your ad is going to be name oriented or need oriented. What is at the top of your ad? If you place your *business name* like a banner across the top of your ad, you are building a *name-oriented* ad. Most businesses tend to do this. After all, it's your business. You are proud of that name. It is what identifies you to the world. It is your Brand.

If the banner instead declares *what you do* or states *the need you fill*, then it is a *need-oriented* ad. When I am helping a client build ads, I make a strong case for using need-oriented ads rather than name orientation. Neither is wrong, but there is a reason I gravitate toward the need-oriented format.

The reason is that, if you think like a customer, especially one who doesn't know about your business yet, your main concern is "who can meet my need?" not "what is the business's name?" When I have a need, I don't care at first what your name is. I just know that I need something and I want to find someone who can supply that need. I'll see your name a second or two later anyway.

If you feel that you want the ad to emphasize branding (name recognition), then you'll want to stay with the name-oriented format.

In an audio script for radio or television, the need/name connection should be very strong. Name repetition and slogan usage should be very tight. Remember that the theme or scenario of the commercial should be geared toward *both* remembering your name *and* the need fulfillment you provide.

If your commercial is only memorable because of the humor in it or some visual and it does not reinforce your name recognition (branding), it will miss the boat. I am sure that millions of dollars are wasted each year on clever television ads where the general content of the ad is remembered but the branding of the advertised company is forgotten.

Consider how you are going to start your ad by building it from the top (or for audiovisual, from the beginning) down. Decide whether you want your branding or your benefit to the customer to be the prominent factor in your ad.

Next, decide how you are going to gain the trust of your potential customers. After all, who hasn't heard the horror stories of people who hired someone to do work, only to have them never do the work or leave it unfinished or do shoddy work and then disappear or create a legal nightmare in trying to resolve the problem?

You need to be able to vouch for yourself and build credibility in the minds of strangers who are considering doing business with you. Unless, of course, you *are* a lying, cheating thief—in which case, please put this book down until you decide to walk the straight and narrow way and are worthy of learning the great gems of wisdom to be found in these pages. Otherwise, may all the people you have swindled or treated dishonestly converge upon you in a dark alley and visit their vengeance on you in ways too horrible to imagine.

At any rate, getting back to our subject, you need to include information to give people a level of comfort in dealing with you. Standing behind your product or your work, resolving any issues that arise, being courteous and polite, acting as a true business professional—somehow you need to communicate that this is the kind of businessperson you are. Tell the truth about why a person should do business with you.

These facts about you are known as "confidence factors." There are many ways to include confidence factors. Are you a member of the BBB or the local chamber of commerce? Are you affiliated with any professional associations relating to your service or product? Are you certified or licensed for what you do?

I have a little more idea than the average consumer about what the "ASE Certified" label means when I see it in an auto repair ad. Most people have no clue what it means. Nonetheless, they know it has something to do with the competency and professional ability of the mechanics, so it becomes a confidence factor. Whether those things are demonstrably true or not, a shop with such certification will be considered more competent and trustworthy than a shop that lacks the identification. That's just the way it is.

Are you rated well on any of the independent sources for business information like Angie's List? How about testimonials from satisfied customers? Have you been in business for a long time? For whatever reason, the decade milepost seems to be the first respected time length for longevity in most businesses. If you haven't been in business for at least ten years, you probably don't want to use your longevity as a confidence factor. Any of these points are good confidence factors, and you should include some in your ad.

People often look for specific product brands. If you carry or service certain brands, it is a good idea to make mention of them. If possible, use the logos of those brands.

Check with your suppliers for the brands to see if they have a co-op program for advertising. Co-op programs are agreements whereby a company will pay a portion of your ad cost when you include their logo and/or slogan in your ad. Since you are helping them brand their products, they may be willing to help pay the bill. The programs vary regarding the specific terms, and these programs come and go and morph all the time, so discuss co-op with your suppliers. It's worth checking out.

What is the extent of your service? Do you service all brands and makes or do you specialize in certain ones? As a potential customer, I want to know whether you can repair my particular product.

Are you available for emergency service? Can I reach you 24/7? Or are you available only eight to five on Mondays through Fridays? Or maybe you are available by appointment only. I need to know this to determine whether I should call you or not. Don't make me call to find out. You will be wasting my valuable time.

How about service areas? If you travel to your customers, how far out are you willing to go? Are there certain communities or areas you especially want to include? Better mention them.

If you have a shop or store location, include a map and/or directional information so I can easily find you. If you have the capability, consider including a photo of your storefront.

Your ad should urge me to give you a call or to make the trip to your store. Make it worth my time to do so. What kind of offer can you make me to entice me to call or come by? This is referred to as the "call to action" and should be included in some way in every ad you do. It may be as simple as "Call Us Today!" or "For Immediate Service, Call ..." or "Don't Spend Another Day Putting Up With..., Come See Us Today!" It may take the form of a limited-time offer or sale. The stronger the call to action, the more likely it is to generate a call or a visit.

When the ad permits artwork, make sure you use the opportunity to the fullest advantage. The pictures or photos you use should immediately identify the subject of your ad and should be relevant to the message you are communicating. It's nice that you have attractive kids, but unless you have them doing something that has to do with your business, save the family photos for the family album.

On the other hand, a photo of you or your crew, dressed appropriately for your type of business, smiling and looking like you are ready to meet the customer, will do much to put your customer at ease and make them feel like they know what to expect.

Make full and ample use of your logo, and publish it in your company color(s) if possible. Also be sure to include any slogan or tag line information on a consistent basis. This is all part of branding your business.

AD PLACEMENT

If your advertising medium has headings like newspaper classifieds or the back sections of some magazines or in yellow pages, make sure you cover as many of those headings with your information as you can. Determine which of the headings apply to your business. Then make yourself a list of the headings and number them from one on down in order of priority. Prioritize them from the one(s) you absolutely *must* appear under to categories representing smaller segments of your business, placing the largest ads under the top-priority headings.

Let's look at a hypothetical example. Suppose you own a beauty salon. You offer the usual haircuts, perms, styling, etc., but in addition you have a nail tech for manicures, nail care, and pedicures. So the headings you would be choosing to appear under might be Beauty Salons, Nail Salons, Hair Stylists, Manicures, and Pedicures. This will depend on the media you are using, but in general, headings like these would be found in places like the yellow pages.

Once you have determined the headings related to what you do, you will list them in order of priority. Obviously, based on the description I gave, you would put Beauty Salons first. Then, perhaps, Hair Styling (or Stylists), and then maybe Nail Salons, followed by Manicures and then Pedicures.

Determine the maximum ad space you can afford and cover as many of the highest-priority headings with the largest-size ads per category that you can afford. That way you'll be sure to have your strongest presence under the heading(s) most important to you, and if you are able to cover a few other headings of less importance, all the better. You may want to adjust this general rule somewhat if the competition under a lesser but still important heading dictates that you need to have a larger presence there to run with the big dogs.

Going back to our beauty salon example, you might find that with the amount you have budgeted for this advertising, you can get a quarter-page ad and maybe a couple of smaller ads. So your flagship ad, the quarter page ad, will go under Beauty Salons. One of your smaller ads might go under Nail Salons, and the other small ad could go under, say, Manicures. You would then try to cover the other headings with a simple listing.

If you find most of your competitors have ads the Hair Stylist heading, you might want to choose to place one of the smaller ads there instead of under a nail-related heading. This will depend on the emphasis you have on the line of service. So there is leeway in prioritizing your business's exposure.

For online placement, consider search-engine marketing in pay-per-click ad programs such as Google adwords. Also consider search-engine optimization for coverage in the organic portion of search-engine results pages. In either case, focus on appropriate keyword units so that your site will appear in appropriate searches.

And don't forget to get yourself listed on local search vehicles such as www.yp.com, www.yellowbook.com, www.superpages.com, etc. These sources are often referenced by major search engines. You will see them listed in the search results on Google, Yahoo!, etc., so make sure you can be found on them. Your local yellow-page companies should have an online local search vehicle, so contact them to find out what kind of listings and profile programs they have. Think of these sources as ads and make sure your profiles on these sources have the same kind of information that your print ads do.

MEASURING AND MAXIMIZING YOUR RESULTS

TRACKING YOUR RESULTS

You will certainly want to know what your advertising does for your business. You will want to have an accurate idea of how many leads your advertising brought you, how much a new customer is worth to you over, say, a year's time, and how well you convert leads to customers. You are going to know this by expending the effort to track your results.

If you track your advertising by using a questionnaire, make sure you ask the right questions. Instead of just asking, "Where did you hear about us?" be more specific. Create a checklist of all the media you use. Then ask, "Which of the following sources influenced your decision to do business with us? Check *all* that apply." Remember that your advertising choices will work *together* rather than in isolation, so you will want to know which ones have worked the most and in what combination.

As you see the answers come in, you should see that some media may be chosen on your tracking form more than others, but you will find that a mix of sources was used. For example, I may see your billboard for months before it has an effect on me. Then I may hear your jingle on the radio enough times to again bring your business to my mind. And maybe, nearer to my time of need, someone mentions that you do a good job at whatever it is I need. That is three forms of creative advertising that have had an influence on my decision.

Finally, when I am ready to take action and do business, I go to a directional source to contact you or come by. So all in all, when you ask your customer how he or she heard about you, they may only mention the word-of-mouth referral, when in actuality, four different media worked together to bring you that customer. If you feel you need to revise your advertising mix, you will have a more dependable guide to determine which media to drop or modify. This is good. This is healthy. This indicates that your advertising campaign is working as effectively as possible.

Ask your advertising sales rep what ways they offer to give you a dependable and complete report of the responses (leads) their advertising products bring you. You will need this information for estimating your return on investment (ROI), the formula we covered earlier in this book.

Some media may offer a tracking phone number. This is a phone number different from your original number. It will appear only in the forms of advertising the ad company is doing for you. The calls from this number roll right to your original number, but in so doing, all the information about the call, including date, time, and duration is tabulated. There may also be access to the person's name and phone number if there is no security block on the customer's number. You may also find that call recording is available, which means that you will be able to go online through a secure portal and actually listen to the content of your calls. In this way, you can remove all doubt about just how many leads were generated.

CONVERTING LEADS INTO CUSTOMERS

The best advertising program in the world will not result in the number of sales you desire unless you do your part to make sure the leads you are generating become customers. Here are a few things you can do to improve the ratio of leads you convert to customers.

Make sure your initial contact with the lead is positive and professional. First, let's consider some simple phone-answering rules.

Your lead should never hear a busy signal. Have a roll-over line or arrange for your primary business phone to forward to your cell, and try to answer every call. It may be unavoidable to have some of your calls go to voice mail, but fight to keep this from happening. Program yourself to think that every call that isn't answered by a live person will be lost. This isn't necessarily the case every time, but if you train yourself to think that way, you'll be more prone to do all you can to prevent lost calls.

Many people don't want to talk to a machine or to voice mail, so an answering service is another possible alternative. The companies providing this service will arrange to have someone take your calls when you are unavailable and will hold the message for you to retrieve or call you on your cell to let you know about the call. This will help to some degree, but I know from my own personal experience that it can be frustrating. There have been times when I have called a company and begun to tell the person on the phone about the reason for my call only to be told that the person I am talking to is only the answering service. Sometimes this is okay. Sometimes it is not.

Regardless, if the caller doesn't talk to a live individual who can provide the needed information, a percentage of those leads will call someone else. If the caller is able to talk to a live individual but is only able to leave a message, a smaller percentage of those leads will be lost. The best policy is to have someone knowledgeable answer every call.

You would not believe the number of times I have called a small business only to hear the digital default voice message declaring, "The number you have called, 444-333-2211, is not available. Please leave a message." Or "Hi, this is Buffy. I can't come to the phone right now ..." Or, when I *do* get a live person, I am greeted with "Hello?" I usually will respond to this last contact with "Oh. Sorry. I may have a wrong number. I was trying to reach a business called Smith Enterprises." Your caller should never have to pry the name of your business out of you. If you use your personal cell phone as your business line, get used to answering every unidentified call with your business name.

Your leads expect to hear a business-like response on the other end of the phone. Think of the well-established businesses you have called. How did they answer their phone? There are a lot of variables in the response, but the common element is that the business name is mentioned:

"Acme Auto Shop."

"Good morning, Dewey, Cheatum & Howe. This is Melissa. How may I direct your call?"

"Bob's Pets. May I help you?"

"Harry's Roofing. This is Harry."

When you answer with your business name, be sure to speak clearly and slowly enough that the caller can understand your business name. It is very frustrating to call a business and have the person on the other end rattle the name of the business off so rapidly that you have to ask the person to repeat it. If you find people asking you what you just said, it is probably because you are talking too fast. Yes, it is tiresome to say the same business name on each call, but remember that this is the first time the caller has heard your name. Be proud enough of it to want it to be understood.

THE POWERFUL EFFECT OF ETHICAL CONDUCT

The next few items of advice are to keep you from unnecessarily losing the impact of your advertising due to ethical problems. Don't hinder or jeopardize your efforts to attract customers by having poor business practices that can speak much louder than the words, slogans, logos, and jingles you use to build the image of your business. Negative press, even in small amounts, tends to outweigh positive image building. If people have bad experiences dealing with you, your top-notch advertising campaign may fall on deaf ears and blind eyes.

Online negative reviews are more and more influential in the shaping of your business reputation. Once posted, these comments can have a detrimental effect on your business. They are not easily counteracted, so pay heed to these few tips and pointers.

If you have a problem with vulgarity, lose it when talking business. Even if your customer or potential customer uses foul language, I advise you not to mirror it. Keep it clean. There is never any call to offend someone just because you feel it is your right to speak your mind, no matter how vulgar. Why lose business just because you can't keep a professional, reasonable, and polite tongue in your head? If you have employees, make sure you train them about this too, since they are your representatives.

It doesn't matter whether you have a third-grade education or a doctorate, whether you wear a suit or a T-shirt, or whether you are a large company or a one-person operation. You are on a totally level playing field when it comes to your ability to sound professional during your phone contact with potential customers. It is up to you to make sure you don't blow a sale by mishandling a phone call.

Next, consider in-person contacts with your leads. When someone walks into your place of business or when you present yourself to someone who has responded to your advertising, how do you treat them?

Believe it or not, I have seen some pretty rude behavior from some businesspeople over the years. Arguing employees, inattentive or seemingly disinterested shop owners, mean-spirited or foul-mouthed business owners, and dirty and/or smelly workers are a

SENSIBLE SMALL BUSINESS ADVERTISING 129

few of the more common ways potential customers can be driven away.

I once dealt with a moving company run by a young husband and wife. The wife was the person who took the incoming calls for the business. I had heard her speaking to callers enough to know that their standard rate for moving was $75 per hour with a three-hour minimum. On one call, however, I heard her speaking to an elderly woman who had only a few things to move, since she was downsizing into an assisted-living apartment. In dealing with the elderly woman, the wife asked the lady her age and then offered the woman a senior discount. She said that their standard rate was $85 an hour but she was going to give her a special senior discount of $10 off! She jacked the rate up so she could appear to give a discount when, in fact, none was given.

I have witnessed contractors who have done the same thing by making coupon or discount offers and then increasing the price of the job by enough to offset the "discount." These are examples of unethical behavior. If you don't see any problem with this, I suggest that you examine your mind and soul. I hope you see the problem and will make sure you avoid this type of conduct. I know that these things seem like common sense, but I have seen every one of these problems played out in real life. Your business should be synonymous with courtesy, professionalism, civility, amiability, and honesty.

Dress appropriately for your line of work. I recommend that if you are a service provider, you consider having some sort of uniform, even if it consists of a screen-printed T-shirt or embroidered jacket. This falls under the category of creative advertising, since you and your workers are walking, talking billboards. For most types of businesses, sexy or revealing clothing is inappropriate. I know, I know. Some of the salespeople you confront in your business may violate this policy, but don't stoop to their level. Keep your appearance and your conduct above reproach. A few slips in these areas will harm your company's reputation and can hinder your advertising results.

PLANNING, GROWING, AND PRIORITIZING

Just as there is no single advertising medium that works exactly the same for everyone, so there is no single way to determine exactly which media to use and at what time you should begin employing them.

The nature of your business will dictate much of your plan. If your business is strictly Internet sales or B2B (business-to-business), your advertising mix will differ from storefront or residential-service businesses. Nonetheless, I am going to provide you with a general idea of the type of development your advertising program should have.

Note that in every case, both directional and creative advertising are included. To start your organized advertising program with only directional or creative media is to greatly curtail the success and effectiveness of your efforts. Remember that your goal is to maximize your response and minimize your investment.

So let's start at the beginning of your business. We will assume that you have followed the earlier advice I gave about building your business plan, and you have determined some sort of a budget figure for your advertising. We are also going to assume that you are starting from scratch, with only word of mouth to get you going. Keep in mind that you aren't going to stop the activities you begin in one step when you go to the next level. These should build one on the other.

I'll divide the program's development into three stages or levels:

Level 1 (Shoestring Budget, First Year Start-Up)
Directional:
- Small yellow page ad(s)
- Business profile listings on local and major search engines
- Website (even if one page)

Creative:
- Word of mouth (with customer appreciation rewards for referring customers)
- Hand-delivered flyers to targeted areas
- Occasional and/or special-event local newspaper ads
- Free articles in local newspapers regarding your start-up
- Business cards
- Yard signs
- Profiles on social media such as LinkedIn, Twitter, Facebook, etc.

Level 2 (Second Year in Business or at First Indication That You Are Ready to Grow)
Directional:
- Increased yellow-page ad coverage (more professional-looking ads with greater size and better placement toward the middle or front of your competitors' ads)
- Expanded website with added information, more profit-center pages, and increased optimization

-Enhanced local search visibility by purchasing higher-placement products on local search engines

Creative:

-Newspaper ads with at least the same regularity as before—more if possible

-Local shopper papers

-Envelope mailers such as Val-Pak

-Exhibit booth at expos, fairs, etc. (include promotional items)

-Small-run ad opportunities, such as map ads, chamber of commerce publications, etc.

Level 3 (Established Business, Consistently Making a Profit)

Directional:

-More dominant ad(s) in your yellow-page heading(s)

-Top placement and banner ads on local search engines

-Sponsored-link advertising on the major search engines

-Revising and expanding your website and its keywords, geo-modifiers, and meta data

Creative:

-Creative media maintained, adjusted, and revised as needed

-Radio and/or television commercials

-Billboards

-Direct mail: single piece, demographically targeted

These levels are only examples of ways to develop your advertising campaign. I have not included every possible type of advertising. I don't want you to blindly follow these levels; rather, I want you to see in them the progression from smaller, more-frugal forms to larger, more-aggressive forms.

Don't worry about your larger, more-seasoned competitor and his deep pockets. Just do the best you can to work smarter at building your advertising visibility and take care of your own reputation. Too often I have run across a business owner who has been so intent on making a big opening splash that he ruined his integrity by biting off more advertising commitment than he could pay for.

Don't let this happen to you. Be as aggressive as you can be, but don't let your brag outdistance your budget. Avoid having a flash-in-the-pan, "here today, gone tomorrow" campaign that ends up overreaching your budget. You don't want to be known as a businessperson with whom no one wants to do business because you don't pay your bills.

If you will work at finding the right campaign mix based on the examples in these levels, you'll prevent overspending and you won't overemphasize one form of advertising over another.

BUDGETING FOR YOUR ADVERTISING

There are many methods businesses use in developing a budget. Among these are the percentage of sales method, the market share method, the unit sales method, the competitive parity method, the objective and task method, the all available funds method, and the affordable method. The most commonly used by small businesses is the percentage of sales method. Right now, many of you are probably thinking, *Say what?!* Well, relax. It is not my purpose to educate you in business finance. You will have to decide how you want to set your budget. My job is to get you to think about it and do it. And the part of your budget about which I am most concerned is the portion of your budget you set aside for advertising.

According to the US Small Business Administration, 5 percent of an entrepreneur's gross sales should be budgeted for advertising. Most advertising resources will tell you that 5 to 7 percent of gross sales is the correct amount to budget for advertising, but not everyone agrees. Roy H. Williams, in an article entitled, "Calculating Your Ad Budget" (found online at http://www.entrepreneur.com/advertising/adcolumnistroyhwilliams/article54436.html), states that "it simply isn't possible to designate a percentage of gross sales for advertising without taking into consideration the markup on your average sale and your rent."

Susan M. Jacksack, a staff writer for CCH Business Owner's Toolkit, notes that spending for promotion, advertising, and even public relations can vary from business to business anywhere from 1 percent (industrial business to business) to more than 10 percent (consumer goods sales).

Variations in spending will also depend on the life cycle of your company, with spending being as high as 50 percent of estimated net sales for first-year start-ups, dropping to 8 percent–10 percent in subsequent years. Budget amounts for retail establishments are known to average around 4 to 6 percent.

I know of one heating and cooling company that sets their advertising budget figure at 4 percent and never varies from it. Whether they do more business or less, that is their stand-pat percentage. Could they benefit from increasing that figure? Probably, but at least they are set at a budget amount to which they are committed regardless of economic downturns. Too many businesses are prone to lower their budget as a panic reaction to a bad economy. Don't do it! Remember the section you read earlier about the example of advertising results during the Great Depression. Those who don't learn from history are doomed to repeat it.

Often, small businesses estimate everything else in their budget and anything left is considered available funds for advertising. This is what would be known in technical terms as a *bad idea*. Advertising should never be an afterthought or an option. You have no business without customers, and advertising is your investment in keeping the flow of customers going. As such, it is as much a necessity as any other essential items in your budget.

A more sensible approach for setting your advertising budget is to estimate what your competitors spend and try to at least match that amount. If you are the new kid on the block, you will have to spend more aggressively to establish your market share objective. If you can't match or exceed competitors' investment in advertising, do the best you can.

Steve Sanghi (Nov. 29, 2009, the *Arizona Republic*, www.azcentral .com) observes, "The fact is that the dollars spent on advertising are never enough. It's because there is always more that can be done ... So companies usually set the budget as a percentage of revenue." If this works for you, do it.

My observations are that there is no single formula that fits every business, but setting a realistic budget is a must. For new businesses, advertising should be a prominent part of your start-up costs and should be planned from the very beginning. You should expect to spend the most in creative advertising in the beginning, since your arrival on the scene needs to make a splash and you have to gain the attention needed to brand yourself in the public eye. But make sure you have your directional advertising represented as well.

Businesses who do not budget for advertising are the most reluctant to consider it because they find that they used up whatever start-up funds they had in doing other things, and therefore they have nothing left to spend to promote their business most effectively. Then, when an advertising representative contacts them, they panic, fearing a further drain on their already stretched or nonexistent resources, and they run from the very thing that would help them. Don't get caught in this error.

12

A WORD ABOUT MLMS AND FRANCHISES

There is an old American advertising consultant proverb that says that there are three things that can kill an advertising program quicker than anything else: your accountant, your spouse, or your business partner if he or she wasn't present when you met with your advertising consultant. (Heaven help you if the person I'm referring to holds more than one of those titles.)

The main problem is that the dissenter(s) only see money going out to pay for the advertising program. In most cases, the ad product is somewhat intangible. You don't necessarily see the effect of the program right away, so it is easy for the doubter to feel that the money you want to invest in advertising should go somewhere more "practical." Go back and read the section on the importance of investing in advertising to refresh your memory about how important this step is.

Now on to the real subject of this section. I can't tell you how many people I have talked to in the past regarding their MLM (multilevel-marketing) businesses, such as Amway, Shaklee, Arbonne, etc., or franchises. From health drinks and elixirs to dietary supplements to soaps and cleansers to prepaid legal services to water-purification systems to travel agencies to baubles and trinkets of all kinds, each multilevel-marketing business opportunity presents itself as completely unique when it comes to the possibility of making millions.

Please don't misunderstand me. I have no problem with any business opportunity that has a legitimate product to offer and provides a proven method for making money. If you understand the product or service and you want to give it a go, by all means, have at it.

But be aware that your "upline" or, in the case of franchises, your corporate advisers, may put the brakes on certain forms of advertising. In my estimation, after attempting to deal with these situations, I have found that you will be sledding uphill trying to get their support or clearance to utilize some forms of advertising.

I can understand some of the hesitance from these companies. I talked to a woman whose MLM business sold a certain line of cookware and kitchen utensils. We met, determined her advertising needs, and came up with what would have been some very well-worded, well-placed ads, complete with her company's logo, to be placed in her area phone directory. (This was a few years back, before online advertising was as prominent.) A few days later she called me to say that she had to cancel her ad program at the direction of her "Double-Diamond" upline. The problem? Well, for starters, no one below a certain level in the hierarchy was permitted to use the company logo. And second, she was discouraged from following any means of marketing or advertising that departed from the "each-one-tells-one" recruitment format that just about every MLM uses in some form or another.

One of the reasons for this hesitancy, or even prohibition, against using "unapproved" advertising has to do with the high turnover inherent in these opportunities. If you have ever tried one of these ventures and dropped out after a while, you know what I mean. For me, it was Amway. If you have tried the program and it worked well for you and you have all the yachts, vacations, diamond rings, and fabulous homes you can handle from the business, great.

The simple truth is that the drop-out rate in multilevel-marketing businesses is high. So for any of these businesses, to allow any participant the ability to use their logo in advertising is to risk having the ad direct people to a nonexistent business or to a disgruntled former distributor. It would not speak well of the MLM company to have their logo appearing in an ad when the person who took out the ad has quit the business. The distributor is gone, yet there is the phone number staring people in the face every time they try to contact that company.

So the company guards its image by allowing ad and logo usage only by the truly successful members of the organization who have proven their longevity with the company. This makes sense in light of the circumstances.

The more disturbing part to me is the emphasis placed on limiting the distributor's business exposure to the pyramid-building nature of the business plan. By "pyramid," I am not referring to illegal pyramid schemes. I simply mean the "drawing of circles" (or whatever it may be called) whereby one person invites one or more people to a vaguely described meeting to hear about a unique business opportunity. Apparently any departure from this recruitment method is frowned upon since it might upset the functioning of the upline/downline hierarchy. Personally speaking, I'm not so sure other forms of advertising would really hinder the system.

Again let me emphasize: if that's the way you want to build your business, that's fine. There is nothing wrong with that. But if, in the course of building your business, you are forbidden from running ads or participating in certain forms of advertising, I encourage you not to be a robot by blindly following the dictates of your MLM guru, especially if that means ignoring directional-advertising opportunities. I have yet to hear any substantial reasons for denying MLM members permission to invest in certain forms of advertising. You can still draw your circles and build your hierarchy while using other advertising. The more people you can make aware of the opportunity the better. So why hinder your opportunity?

Similarly, franchise companies often have totalitarian sway over the advertising methods they will allow their franchisees to use. One of the most common mistakes franchises make is to overinvest in creative advertising to the virtual exclusion and detriment of directional advertising.

Take an ice cream parlor franchise for instance. You will see colorful billboards, television commercials, and magazine and newspaper ads tempting you to buy some scrumptious-looking ice cream concoction. The advertising is usually heavy on branding, including the logo, one of the signature dishes, and the company slogan. In some instances, you may see location/phone number information and possibly some kind of call to action such as a buy-one-get-one coupon offer. So far, so good.

One franchise owner told me how the company's corporate office required the franchises throughout a certain metropolitan area to run television commercials produced by the company. The commercials were well done, complete with snappy, fast-moving action, tantalizing product images, and upbeat music. The commercials gave no location, phone number, or special offer information. The franchise owner claimed that the commercials didn't do anything for him. I begged to differ.

Although he didn't see a difference in the traffic into his stores, the commercials weren't necessarily meant to accomplish that. Since they lacked the necessary components to bring a more immediate response, these commercials were designed to increase the top-of-mind awareness (TOMA) of the company and its product line. In and of themselves they were not meant to increase the immediate flow of business. They were meant to create the desire for some delectable ice cream and to brand the company as the place to go to satisfy the desire: branding.

So the commercials *were* doing their job. In this case the franchisee had an incorrect expectation of what the advertising was meant to accomplish. You wouldn't use a screwdriver to hammer nails, nor would you be disappointed in the screwdriver for its failure to do so. The same applies to advertising media. Use them as each is intended to be used, and don't be too disappointed if you have the wrong expectation for what the results are.

I know of another ice cream franchise where their idea of an advertising campaign to attract new customers was to offer a free waffle cone on Tuesdays. The only advertising they did for the offer was to place signs inside the store and on the parlor windows. This is great for reaching customers who are already in the store and, to a lesser extent, a few passers-by, but how in the ever-loving world can this be seen as effective in securing new customers? And just how powerful is a free waffle cone offer anyway? *I* wouldn't go out of *my* way for an offer as weak as that. I just don't get it. Where is the common sense in their marketing department?

Was this the result of a corporate directive or was the decision made on the local franchise level? If it was done on the local franchise level, was the offer so anemic because of corporate restrictions on doing anything more aggressive? Thank goodness I don't have to worry about it, because the business in question isn't a client of mine.

The bottom line for franchisees is that you need to have a clear understanding of the freedoms and limitations your franchise company places upon you. If you feel that a particular advertising idea that would be beneficial to your business is prohibited by the company, try to find some way to go to bat for the idea and be ready to defend your request. At any rate, I recommend that you don't just fall in line unquestioningly.

IDENTIFYING AND AVOIDING SCAMS

Now a word about the danger of scams lurking in the mail, by phone, and sometimes in person. When you first open for business, your business contact information will be disseminated on many online business-profile services. You will begin receiving phone solicitations and e-mails from people wanting you to buy something to help your business.

These offers may be for credit card services, printing supplies, alternative phone service, or whatever. Yes, they can be a nuisance. You have better things to do with your time than listen to a sales pitch for lower-cost toner—especially if you don't even have a printer. Many of these may be legitimate pitches for legitimate products and services.

PHONE SCAMS

You won't be in business long before you will receive a phone call declaring that the caller is just wanting to "verify your business information" for some online or phone-book listing. Be careful.

There are unscrupulous (though not necessarily illegal) companies out there that will want you to think they are working for one of the legitimate phone book or online listing services. Be aware that just because someone identifies themselves as a yellow-page or online yellow-page company, that does not mean that they are representing one of the recognized and legitimate phone book/online search companies with which you should be doing business.

If the solicitation for information comes over the phone, you even need to be careful about answering a question with something as simple as yes, because there have been instances where the conversation is recorded and the caller will then take the recorded yes response and splice that answer into another question you probably won't even be asked. The result may be that they will have a doctored response on a recording of you or one of your workers accepting their offer for a paid listing, ad, or service.

So be leery of phone-call solicitations to check or verify your listing. I don't advise just hanging up on them. Instead, take control of the situation by turning the tables on them. Ask them questions. Get the caller's name, the company name, their address, and their phone number and find out exactly where and how your information is to be used. Then tell them you will call them back once you have verified their authenticity and once you have determined that you want your information to appear. If the caller is not on the level, you won't get the information you request and they will more than likely tire of the game and hang up themselves.

Part of these offers may be a free-trial period during which your listing or profile may be offered without cost for a period of time (thirty days, for example), after which you will be billed unless you cancel. They are anticipating that you will forget to cancel or that you will delay cancelling until it is too late to drop the program. Again, steer clear of tactics like this.

MAIL SCAMS

I once had one of my clients become very upset at me and my company for supposedly mailing her an unauthorized bill for some sort of listing. When she showed me the bill, it became clear that she had fallen for one of the ruses I am talking about. The company name on the bill included the words "Yellow Pages" and included the "walking fingers" logo, but the rest of the name, the address, and all other information in the billing documents revealed that the bill was not from my company at all. In fact, not only did the bill not have my company's logo or address, but the only thing in common between the bill and my company was the word "Yellow."

If we were to turn the clock back a few months earlier, we would have seen my client receive a document in the mail that appeared to be a request to confirm the accuracy of her business name, address, and phone number for publication. The document would have included, in large letters somewhere on the form, the words "THIS IS NOT A BILL." This, coupled with the similarity in name and the popularly recognized walking-fingers logo, were enough to mislead her into thinking that the verification was from one of the legitimate phone book/online search providers in her area.

Additionally, let me explain that the walking-fingers logo was never properly trademarked in the early days of yellow pages, so any company providing any sort of yellow pages may use some form of the logo. Do not be fooled.

Pay attention. Know the companies with whom you do business. Call your ad sales rep or call the company directly if you want to check on the validity of anything that doesn't seem right or that you can't remember signing up for. If you don't open your company's mail and you don't pay the bills yourself, make sure whoever does reads this section of this book to prevent problems.

Having said this, let me caution also against overreacting. The initial response of the client I mentioned was to become angry with my company for allowing the questionable company to exist. She was so upset that, until I explained the situation, she had determined to cancel all her advertising with my company. This would have been unwise, since the ad program she was running at the time was bringing her a consistent supply of business leads.

WALK-IN SCAMS

Another scam to avoid may come in the form of a solicitation by a salesman who walks into your business and offers ad space on maps, placemats, or some other form of print advertising. Although there are legitimate companies providing these products, make sure you check out the company and its salesperson. If they insist on payment in full at the time of sale, slow down and do some research. I have heard of instances when a business fell for this scheme and never saw the product they paid for or heard from the salesperson or company again.

Don't become so gun-shy of the hucksters that you refuse to listen to or invest in the legitimate, effective advertising programs you need to survive and thrive. That is, you'll be getting rid of what is worth keeping while tossing out what you don't want.

ADVERTISING CONSULTANTS: WHO NEEDS 'EM?

Having now read about the advertising opportunities available to you and understanding the general strengths and limitations of each one, you may feel that you still aren't sure whether you can put together an appropriate program for your business. You should now know the difference between directional and creative advertising and be aware that you need to cover both of those areas, but you may still feel overwhelmed or unsure about which media in each category you should use to make the best use of your investment.

That is where advertising consultants can be a valuable asset to your arsenal. Remember the cartoon of the king who was too busy fighting the war to listen to the machine-gun salesman? Well, suppose he had delegated the duty of listening to the salesman to an advisor. Suppose he had chosen his advisor based upon his expertise in the area of weaponry and had entrusted him with the responsibility to determine the best use of his defense budget, choose the best weapons available, and purchase them for the king.

You are the king or queen of your business. You may be like many others in your situation. You know how to run your business, and you truly are too busy to spend the time it takes to develop the most effective ad program. If that is the case, consider delegating the responsibility to someone who knows the field and can do the development and maintenance of the program for you.

I am not talking about blindly assigning it to the least-busy person on your staff or to your spouse just because they are handy. In most cases, they won't have the experience necessary to accomplish the task. In some small business situations, this may be the only thing you can do, since you may be on a shoestring budget and can't afford any other option. The person you designate then has the responsibility to educate him- or herself about advertising and the media available. One of the easiest ways to start the person on the right road is to have him or her read this book.

But for many of you, starting out with a professional advertising consultant will be the most judicious use of your time and money. For many businesses, such as physicians' practices, law offices, auto body and repair shops, light industrial and manufacturing facilities, landscaping companies, etc., the benefits are well worth the investment.

Competent advertising consultants should be aware of everything I have mentioned in this book and will be able to devote the necessary time to the advertising process. They should be aware of the latest developments in the field of advertising. They should have the ability to evaluate advertising opportunities in light of your business and its needs. They will be able to spend the proper amount of time meeting, developing relationships with, and listening to advertising salespeople. They will be able to negotiate for the best offers, bundles, and packages to maximize your budget.

Even if you are not yet to the place in your business growth where you feel you can afford a "hired gun," keep it in mind for your future business development. When you are a very small start-up, this need may seem light years beyond where you are and maybe even beyond where you ever hope to be, but think about it anyway.

The steps in your process may entail the following:

1. Handling all the responsibilities for advertising yourself, including self-education, designating time for advertising representatives, setting the budget, choosing options, tracking and evaluating results, and tweaking the program as you go.

2. Delegating the responsibility to someone else. I know this runs against your grain. Most small business owners have a problem with delegating authority. They want to be in control of every aspect of the business. After all, the outcome may mean the life or death of your business. I understand that. But you do need to be confident that the person running your advertising program has as much interest in the success of your business as you do.

3. When your budget will allow it, hire an advertising consultant or an in-house marketing/advertising director.

If you want someone who deals only with your business, you will want to place the director on the payroll. The most difficult aspect of adding someone to the payroll may be finding one with enough of the right experience, especially if you are trying to hire from within your company.

If you want to hire the services of an outside consultant, someone who represents multiple companies instead of just yours, the experience factor won't be as much of an issue, since these consultants usually have a far-wider base of experience, contacts, and knowledge than your internally assigned advertising director. At any rate, the payoff to you is that you will have someone who can build the best possible program and free you to run the business. You will have more effective ad response, which will mean more leads, which means more customers, which means more work/sales, which means more income, etc.

THE *"READER'S DIGEST"* CONDENSED VERSION

I am a big fan of acronyms because they are a great way to remember information. We've all heard of KISS—Keep It Simple, Stupid.

Here is an acronym that sums up much of what I have taught you in this book. It won't hit everything, and I hope there are many more principles, examples, and guidelines that have stuck in your mind, but remember these gems:

How do you spell **SUCCESS**?

Start Learning about Your Advertising Options

Understand the Difference between Directional and Creative

Advertising (and Use Both)

Constantly Think Like a Customer

Carefully Track Your Results

Establish Good Relationships with Your Ad Salespeople

Set a Realistic Budget for Your Advertising

Specialize Your Advertising Message So That It Stands Out

FINAL THOUGHTS

It is my hope that in these few pages you have gained valuable insight into advertising and that you will be more successful than ever before in your business as a result.

Remember some of the best traits of a good businessperson:

- the humility to admit that you can't know everything

- the resourcefulness to borrow brains from those who know more than you

- the ability to adapt and change

There is more to be learned, especially in the area of online visibility, but if you will follow the advice I have laid out in these few pages, I believe you will be way ahead of your competitors who are still floundering around, trying to make sense of their advertising efforts.

If you have the will to win, if you have the hunger to learn and have maintained a teachable spirit, if you will be diligent about following the advice from the brains you just borrowed, you will run a more efficient, more profitable ad campaign than businesses with far-deeper advertising pockets that lack the focus and the sensibility of the kind of advertising program you will build and run. Throwing more money at a problem isn't always the best way to solve it. Determine a reasonable budget from the very start. Then work smarter, not necessarily harder.

Now that you know how, *go do it!*

INDEX

Page numbers with italicized "*ill*" reference illustrations and diagrams.

logos, company
in ads, 120
on gadgets, 95–97

M

magazines, advertising in, 47, 94
magic bullet in advertising, 33
magnetic signs, advertising with, 85
mail, identifying and avoiding scams
by, 147–48
major search engines, 58–65
management skills, lack of, 9
map-locator functions, 64*ill*
online, 63–64
marketing
importance of advertising and, 10,
42–43
marketing consultant, avoiding conflict
with, 41–43
mechanical billboards, advertising on,
79
meta-tag keywords, website, 108–9
mini ads, indoor, 81–82
mission, of business, 8
MLM (multilevel-marketing)
businesses, 140–44
mobile advertising (on cars or trucks),
84–86
money, as motivation for starting
business, 8
motor vehicles, advertising on, 49,
84–86
Moutray, Chad, 11
movie theater advertising, 94–95
mugs, using company logos on, 95
multilevel-marketing (MLM)
businesses, 140–44

N

name recognition (branding)
in billboard advertising, 80
building, 47
name-oriented ads for, 116–17
rooftop displays and, 86
using pre-movie ads for, 95

using promotional products for, 97
name-oriented ads, 116–17
National Survey of Small Business
Finances (1995), 12
need-oriented ads, 116
negative press, effect of, 127–28
new product mobile advertising, 85
newspapers, advertising in, 47, 51*ill*,
53, 70–73

O

Office of Advocacy, US, on percentage
of small businesses, 11
online
advertising using e-mail, 92–93
commercial, 58
cost of internet advertising, 64–65
coupons, 58
creating business using social
posting sites, 60, 90–92
effect of negative reviews, 128
local community advertising, 99
local search engines, 46, 57–58, 59*ill*
map-locator functions, 63–64, 64*ill*
maps, 63–64
participation in forums, 92
placement of ads, 122
yellow pages, 57–58
online business, cost of, 64–65
Open Sky Media (OSM) Blog,
"Companies That Survived the Great
Depression," 24
Orfalea, Paul, 53
"organic" search section, 61–63, 62*ill*
organizational memberships, 98–99
OSM (Open Sky Media) Blog,
"Companies That Survived the Great
Depression," 24
outdoor signage, advertising with
billboards, 47, 49, 51*ill*, 78–81
bus stop signs, 84
on cars or trucks (mobile
advertising), 49, 84–86
roadside benches, 84
yard signs, 83–84
overexpansion, danger of, 9

on percentage of sales for
advertising, 135–36
on percentage of workers in small
businesses, 11
scams, identifying and avoiding
about, 145–49
by mail, 147–48
by phone, 146–47
by walk-in salespeople, 148–49
SCORE, information on developing
business plan, 8
search engines
local, 46, 57–58, 122
major, 58–65
search-engine
advertising, 59*ill*, 61
ranking, 58–60
Search-Engine-Optimized (SEO)
website, 9, 61, 63, 105, 110, 122
search-results pages, 61
shoestring budget
getting right start on, 45–46
starting advertising program with,
131
starting without sufficient, 9
short-term advertising, 71–72
signage, advertising with
billboards, 47, 49, 78–81
on cars or trucks (mobile
advertising), 49, 51*ill*, 84–86
indoor mini ads, 81–82
roadside benches, 84
yard signs, 83–84
size of ads, 113–14
"skins," vehicle, 85
small business, importance of, 11–12
Small Business Administration (SBA)
on first year survival of small
businesses, 12
on percentage of sales for
advertising budget, 135–36
on percentage of workers in small
businesses, 11
social media, creating business using,
59-60, 90–92
specialty papers, advertising in, 72
sponsored links, search-engine, 61

starting business
first-time at, 4–5
reasons for business failure, 8
start-ups
advertising budget for, 137
need for advertising consultants,
153–54
reason for death of, 8-10
starting advertising program, 131
sticky drives, using for advertising, 97
SUCCESS, advertising, 155–56

T
teachable, being, 10
team, forming marketing, 41–43
telemarketing, 73–74
telephone
getting tracking number, 124–25
responses from advertising, 125–27
scams, 146–47
sounding professional to contacts,
128
television, advertising on, 28, 47, 49,
51*ill*, 75–76
thinking
like potential customer, 21–22
outside of the box, 34
Thomas, Russ, 6–7
title meta tags, website, 107–109
TOMA (Top-Of-Mind Awareness), 47,
51*ill*, 79, 81, 143
top placement listings, Internet, 57
Top-Of-Mind Awareness (TOMA), 47,
51*ill*, 79, 81, 143
tracking phone number, getting,
124–25
tracking results, ROI and, 32–33,
123–25
trucks, advertising on, 49, 84–86
Twain, Mark, 71
Twitter, creating business using, 90–92